Microsoft® Excel 5.0

for Windows™
Illustrated Brief Edition

Elizabeth Eisner Reding

Course Technology, Inc. One Main Street, Cambridge, MA 02142

An International Thomson Publishing Company

Albany • Bonn • Boston • Cincinnati • London • Madrid • Melbourne • Mexico City
New York • Paris • San Francisco • Singapore • Tokyo • Toronto • Washington

Microsoft Excel 5.0 for Windows — Illustrated Brief Edition is published by Course Technology, Inc.

Managing Editor:	Marjorie Hunt
Product Manager:	Nicole Jones Pinard
Production Supervisor:	Kathryn Dinovo
Text Designer:	Leslie Hartwell
Cover Designer:	John Gamache

©1995 Course Technology, Inc.
A Division of International Thomson Publishing, Inc.

For more information contact:
Course Technology, Inc.
One Main Street
Cambridge, MA 02142

International Thomson Publishing Europe
Berkshire House 168-173
High Holborn
London WCIV 7AA
England

International Thomson Publishing GmbH
Königswinterer Strasse 418
53227 Bonn
Germany

Thomas Nelson Australia
102 Dodds Street
South Melbourne, 3205
Victoria, Australia

International Thomson Publishing Asia
211 Henderson Road
#05-10 Henderson Building
Singapore 0315

Nelson Canada
1120 Birchmount Road
Scarborough, Ontario
Canada M1K 5G4

International Thomson Publishing Japan
Hirakawacho Kyowa Building, 3F
2-2-1 Hirakawacho
Chiyoda-ku, Tokyo 102
Japan

International Thomson Editores
Campos Eliseos 385, Piso 7
Col. Polanco
11560 Mexico D.F. Mexico

Trademarks

Course Technology and the open book logo are registered trademarks of Course Technology, Inc.

I (T) P The ITP logo is a trademark under license.

Some of the product names in this book have been used for identification purposes only and may be trademarks or registered trademarks of their respective manufacturers and sellers.

Disclaimer

Course Technology, Inc. reserves the right to revise this publication and make changes from time to time in its content without notice.

ISBN 0-7600-3501-6

Printed in the United States of America

10 9 8 7 6 5 4 3 2

From the Publisher

At Course Technology, Inc., we believe that technology will transform the way that people teach and learn. We are very excited about bringing you, instructors and students, the most practical and affordable technology-related products available.

The Course Technology Development Process

Our development process is unparalleled in the educational publishing industry. Every product we create goes through an exacting process of design, development, review, and testing.

Reviewers give us direction and insight that shape our manuscripts and bring them up to the latest standards. Every manuscript is quality tested. Students whose background matches the intended audience work through every keystroke, carefully checking for clarity and pointing out errors in logic and sequence. Together with our technical reviewers, these testers help us ensure that everything that carries our name is as error free and easy to use as possible.

Course Technology Products

We show both *how* and *why* technology is critical to solving problems in the classroom and in whatever field you choose to teach or pursue. Our time-tested, step-by-step instructions provide unparalleled clarity. Examples and applications are chosen and crafted to motivate students.

The Course Technology Team

This book will suit your needs because it was delivered quickly, efficiently, and affordably. In every aspect of business, we rely on a commitment to quality and the use of technology. Every employee contributes to this process. The names of all our employees are listed below: Tim Ashe, David Backer, Stephen M. Bayle, Josh Bernoff, Ann Marie Buconjic, Jody Buttafoco, Kerry Cannell, Jim Chrysikos, Barbara Clemens, Amy Clemons, Susan Collins, John M. Connolly, Kim Crowley, Myrna D'Addario, Lisa D'Alessandro, Jodi Davis, Howard S. Diamond, Kathryn Dinovo, Joseph B. Dougherty, Laurie Duncan, Karen Dwyer, MaryJane Dwyer, Kristin Dyer, Chris Elkhill, Don Fabricant, Viktor Frengut, Jeff Goding, Laurie Gomes, Eileen Gorham, Catherine Griffin, Tim Hale, Jamie Harper, Roslyn Hooley, John Hope, Marjorie Hunt, Matt Kenslea, Susannah Lean, Kim Mai, Margaret Makowski, Tammy Marciano, Elizabeth Martinez, Debbie Masi, Don Maynard, Dan Mayo, Kathleen McCann, Sarah McLean, Jay McNamara, Mac Mendelsohn, Karla Mitchell, Kim Munsell, Amy Oliver, Michael Ormsby, Debbie Parlee, Kristin Patrick, Charlie Patsios, Darren Perl, Kevin Phaneuf, George J. Pilla, Nicole Jones Pinard, Cathy Prindle, Nancy Ray, Laura Sacks, Carla Sharpe, Deborah Shute, Jennifer Slivinski, Christine Spillett, Michelle Tucker, David Upton, Mark Valentine, Karen Wadsworth, Renee Walkup, Tracy Wells, Donna Whiting, Janet Wilson, Lisa Yameen.

Preface

Course Technology, Inc. is proud to present this new book in its Illustrated Series. *Microsoft Excel 5.0 for Windows — Illustrated Brief Edition* provides a highly visual, hands-on introduction to Microsoft Excel. The book is designed as a learning tool for Excel novices but will also be useful as a source for future reference. It assumes students have learned basic Windows skills and file management from *Microsoft Windows 3.1 — Illustrated Brief Edition* or from an equivalent book.

Organization and Coverage

Microsoft Excel 5.0 for Windows — Illustrated Brief Edition contains four units that cover basic Excel skills. In these units students learn how to plan, define, create, and modify worksheets. They also chart the data and learn how to add enhancements such as text annotations and arrows.

Approach

Microsoft Excel 5.0 for Windows — Illustrated Brief Edition distinguishes itself from other textbooks with its highly visual approach to computer instruction.

Lessons: Information Displays

The basic lesson format of this text is the "information display," a two-page lesson that is sharply focused on a specific task. This sharp focus and the precise beginning and end of a lesson make it easy for students to study specific material. Modular lessons are less overwhelming for students, and they provide instructors with more flexibility in planning classes and assigning specific work. The units are modular as well and can be presented in any order.

Each lesson, or "information display," contains the following elements:

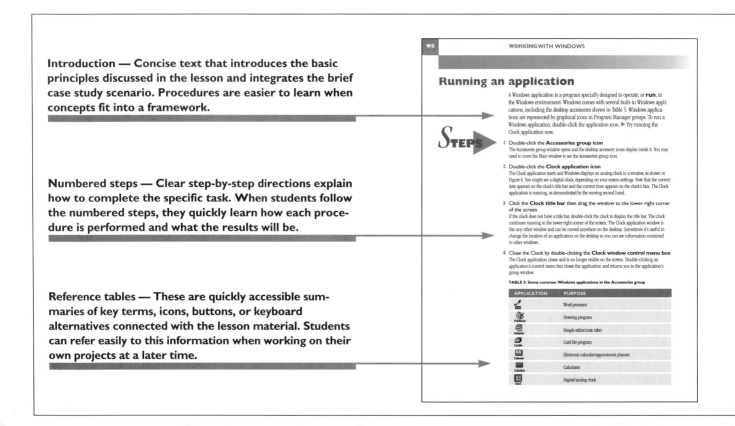

Introduction — Concise text that introduces the basic principles discussed in the lesson and integrates the brief case study scenario. Procedures are easier to learn when concepts fit into a framework.

Numbered steps — Clear step-by-step directions explain how to complete the specific task. When students follow the numbered steps, they quickly learn how each procedure is performed and what the results will be.

Reference tables — These are quickly accessible summaries of key terms, icons, buttons, or keyboard alternatives connected with the lesson material. Students can refer easily to this information when working on their own projects at a later time.

Features

Microsoft Excel 5.0 for Windows — Illustrated Brief Edition is an exceptional textbook because it contains the following features:

- "Read This Before You Begin Microsoft Excel 5.0" Page — This page provides essential information that both students and instructors need to know before they begin working through the units.

- Real-World Case — The case study used throughout the textbook is designed to be "real-world" in nature and representative of the kinds of activities that students will encounter when working with spreadsheet software. With a real-world case, the process of learning skills will be more meaningful to students.

- End of Unit Material — Each unit concludes with a meaningful Concepts Review that tests students' understanding of what they learned in the unit. The Concepts Review is followed by an Applications Review, which provides students with additional hands-on practice of the skills they learned in the unit. The Applications Review is followed by Independent Challenges, which pose case problems for students to solve. The Independent Challenges allow students to learn by exploring and develop critical thinking skills.

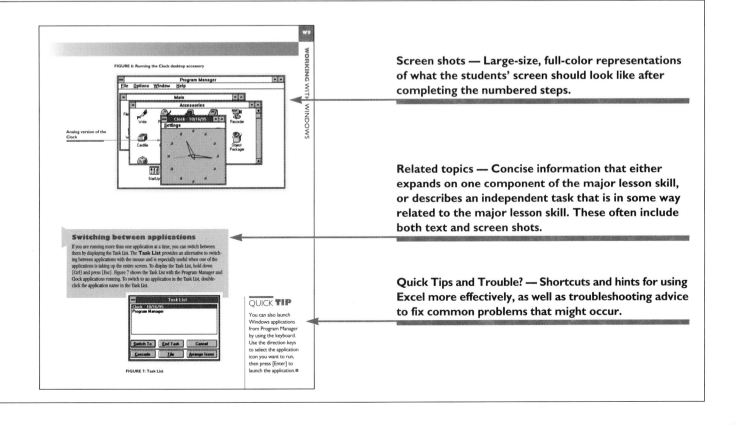

The Student Disk

The Student Disk bundled with the instructor's copy of this book contains all the data files students need to complete the step-by-step lessons.

Adopters of this text are granted the right to post the Student Disk on any standalone computer or network used by students who have purchased this product.

For more information on the Student Disk, see the page in this book called "Read This Before You Begin Microsoft Excel 5.0."

The Supplements

Instructor's Manual — The Instructor's Manual is quality assurance tested. It includes:

- Solutions to all lessons, Concept Reviews, Application Reviews, and Independent Challenges
- A disk containing solutions to all of the lessons, Concept Reviews, Application Reviews, and Independent Challenges
- Unit notes, which contain tips from the author about the instructional progression of each lesson
- Extra problems
- Transparency masters of key concepts

Test Bank — The Test Bank contains approximately 50 questions per unit in true/false, multiple choice, and fill-in-the-blank formats, plus two essay questions. Each question has been quality assurance tested by students to achieve clarity and accuracy.

Electronic Test Bank — The Electronic Test Bank allows instructors to edit individual test questions, select questions individually or at random, and print out scrambled versions of the same test to any supported printer.

Acknowledgments

This book was made possible due to the extreme persistence and devotion of the Course Technology team, especially Nicole Jones Pinard, Kitty Pinard, Marjorie Hunt, and Kathryn Dinovo.

I would also like to acknowledge my Dad, who instilled in me the qualities of drive, attention to detail, and personal integrity.

Elizabeth Eisner Reding

Contents

Microsoft Excel 5.0
for Windows™

Read This Before You Begin
Microsoft Excel 5.0

To the Student

The lessons and exercises in this book feature several Excel workbook files provided to your instructor. To complete the step-by-step lessons, Applications Reviews, and Independent Challenges in this book, you must have a Student Disk. Your instructor will do one of the following: 1) provide you with your own copy of the disk; 2) have you copy it from the network onto your own floppy disk; or 3) have you copy the lesson files from a network into your own subdirectory on the network. Always use your own copies of the lesson and exercise files. See your instructor or technical support person for further information.

Using Your Own Computer

If you are going to work through this book using your own computer, you need a computer system running Microsoft Windows 3.1, Microsoft Excel 5.0 for Windows, and a Student Disk. *You will not be able to complete the step-by-step lessons in this book using your own computer until you have your own Student Disk.* This book assumes the default settings under a Standard installation of Microsoft Excel 5.0 for Windows.

To the Instructor

Bundled with the instructor's copy of this book is a Student Disk. The Student Disk contains all the files your students need to complete the step-by-step lessons in the units, Applications Reviews, and Independent Challenges. As an adopter of this text, you are granted the right to distribute the files on the Student Disk to any student who has purchased a copy of the text. You are free to post all of these files to a network or standalone workstations, or simply provide copies of the disk to your students. The instructions in this book assume that the students know which drive and directory contain the Student Disk, so it's important that you provide disk location information before the students start working through the units. This book also assumes that Excel 5.0 is set up using the Standard installation procedure.

Using the Student Disk Files

To keep the original files on the Student Disk intact, the instructions in this book for opening files require two important steps: (1) open the existing file and (2) save it as a new file with a new name. This procedure ensures that the original file will remain unmodified in case the student wants to redo any lesson or exercise.

To organize their files, students are instructed to save their files to the MY_FILES directory on their Student Disk that they created in *Microsoft Windows 3.1*. In case your students did not complete this lesson, it is included in the Instructor's Manual that accompanies this book. You can circulate this to your students, or you can instruct them to simply save to drive A or drive B.

UNIT 1

Getting Started

WITH MICROSOFT EXCEL 5.0

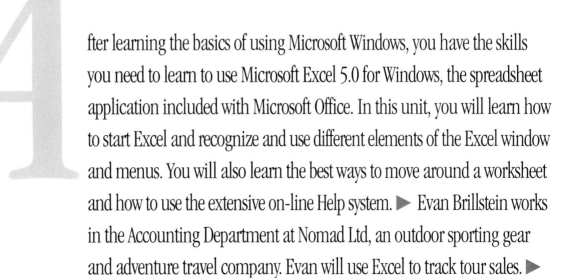

After learning the basics of using Microsoft Windows, you have the skills you need to learn to use Microsoft Excel 5.0 for Windows, the spreadsheet application included with Microsoft Office. In this unit, you will learn how to start Excel and recognize and use different elements of the Excel window and menus. You will also learn the best ways to move around a worksheet and how to use the extensive on-line Help system. ▶ Evan Brillstein works in the Accounting Department at Nomad Ltd, an outdoor sporting gear and adventure travel company. Evan will use Excel to track tour sales. ▶

Defining spreadsheet software

Excel is an electronic spreadsheet that runs on Windows computers. An **electronic spreadsheet** uses a computer to perform numeric calculations rapidly and accurately. See Table 1-1 for common ways spreadsheets are used in business. An electronic spreadsheet is also referred to as a **worksheet**, which is the document that you produce when you use Excel. A worksheet created with Excel allows Evan to work quickly and efficiently, and the result produced will be accurate and easily updated. He will be able to produce more professional-looking documents. Figure 1-1 shows a budget worksheet that Evan created using pencil and paper. Figure 1-2 shows the same worksheet that Evan can create using Excel.

Excel is better than the paper system for the following reasons:

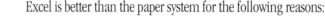

Enter data quickly and accurately
With Excel, Evan can enter information faster and more accurately than he could using the pencil and paper method. He needs to enter only data and formulas, and Excel calculates the results.

Recalculate easily
Fixing errors using Excel is easy, and any results based on a changed entry are recalculated automatically.

Perform What-if Analysis
One of the most powerful decision-making features of Excel is the ability to change data and then quickly recalculate changed results. Anytime you use a worksheet to answer the question "what if," you are performing a what-if analysis. For instance, if the advertising budget for May were increased to $3,000, Evan could enter the new figure into the spreadsheet and immediately find out the impact on the overall budget.

Change the appearance of information
Excel provides powerful features for enhancing a spreadsheet so that information is visually appealing and easy to understand.

Create charts
Excel makes it easy to create charts based on information in a worksheet. With Excel, charts are automatically updated as data changes. The worksheet in Figure 1-2 includes a pie chart that graphically shows the distribution of expenses for the second quarter.

Share information with other users
Because everyone at Nomad is now using Microsoft Office, it's easy for Evan to share information with his colleagues. If Evan wants to use the data from someone else's worksheet, he accesses their files through the network or by disk.

Create new worksheets from existing ones quickly
It's easy for Evan to take an existing Excel worksheet and quickly modify it to create a new one.

FIGURE 1-1:
Traditional paper
worksheet

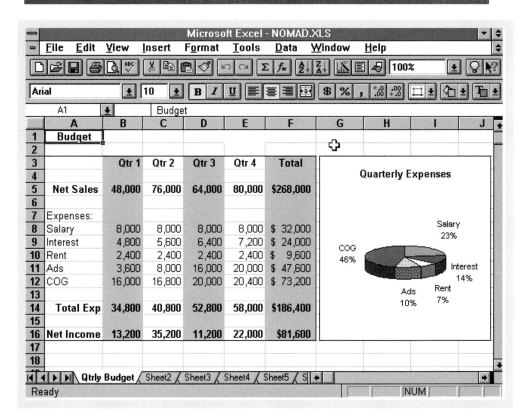

Nomad Ltd

	Qtr 1	Qtr 2	Qtr 3	Qtr 4	Total
Net Sales	48,000	76,000	64,000	80,000	268,000
Expenses:					
Salary	8,000	8,000	8,000	8,000	32,000
Interest	4,800	5,600	6,400	7,200	24,000
Rent	2,400	2,400	2,400	2,400	9,600
Ads	3,600	8,000	16,000	20,000	47,600
COG	16,000	16,800	20,000	20,400	73,200
Total Exp	34,800	40,800	52,800	58,000	186,400
Net Income	13,200	35,200	11,200	22,000	81,600

FIGURE 1-2:
Excel worksheet

TABLE 1-1: Common business spreadsheet uses

USE	SOLUTION
Maintenance of values	Calculation of figures
Visual representation of values	Chart based on worksheet figures

Starting Excel 5.0 for Windows

To start Excel, you first start Windows, as described in "Microsoft Windows 3.1." Then you open the Microsoft Office program group window that contains the Microsoft Excel application icon. A slightly different procedure might be required for computers on a network and those that use utility programs to enhance Windows. If you need assistance, ask your instructor or technical support person for help. ▶ Evan starts Excel now.

1   **Make sure the Program Manager window is open**
The Program Manager icon might appear at the bottom of your screen. Double-click it to open it, if necessary.

2   **Double-click the Microsoft Office program group icon**
The Microsoft Office group window opens, displaying the Microsoft Excel icon and other Microsoft applications as shown in Figure 1-3. Your desktop might look different depending on the applications installed on your computer. The Microsoft Office group icon on your screen might already be maximized. If you cannot locate the Microsoft Office program icon, click Window on the Program Manager menu bar, then click Microsoft Office.

3   **Double-click the Microsoft Excel application icon**
Excel opens and a blank worksheet appears. In the next lesson, you will familiarize yourself with the elements of the Excel worksheet window.

FIGURE 1-3: Microsoft Office program icon group

Microsoft Excel application icon

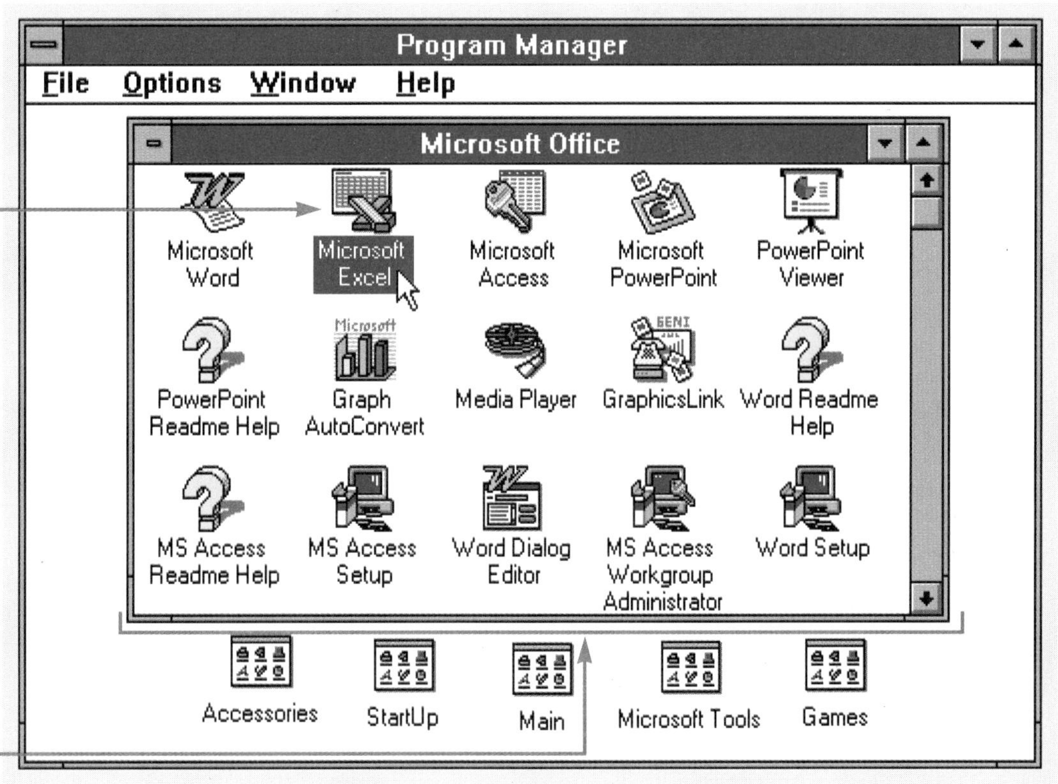

List of available applications might vary

TROUBLE?

If you don't have a Microsoft Office program group icon, look for one called Microsoft Excel.■

Viewing the Excel window

When you start Excel, the computer displays the **worksheet window**, the area where you enter data, and the window elements that enable you to create and work with worksheets. Familiarize yourself with the Excel worksheet window and its elements by comparing the descriptions below to Figure 1-4.

■ The **worksheet window** contains a grid of columns and rows. Columns are labeled alphabetically (A, B, C, etc.) and rows are labeled numerically (1, 2, 3 etc.). The worksheet window displays only a tiny fraction of the whole worksheet, which has a total of 256 columns and 16,384 rows. The intersection of a column and a row is a **cell**. Cells can contain text, numbers, formulas, or a combination of all three. Every cell has its own unique location or **cell address**, which is identified by the coordinates of the intersecting column and row. For example, the cell address of the cell in the upper-left corner of a worksheet is A1.

■ The **cell pointer** is a dark rectangle that highlights the cell you are working in, or the **active cell**. In Figure 1-4, the cell pointer is located at A1, so A1 is the active cell. To make another cell active, click any other cell or press the arrow keys on your keyboard to move the cell pointer.

■ The **title bar** displays the application name (Microsoft Excel) and the filename of the open worksheet (in this case, Book1). The title bar also contains a control menu box and resizing buttons, which you learned about in "Microsoft Windows 3.1."

■ The **menu bar** contains menus from which you choose Excel commands. As with all Windows applications, you can choose a menu command by clicking it with the mouse or by pressing [Alt] plus the underlined letter in the menu name.

■ The **name box** displays the active cell address. In Figure 1-4, "A1" appears in the name box, which means that A1 is the active cell.

■ The **formula bar** allows you to enter or edit data in the worksheet.

■ The **toolbars** contain buttons for the most frequently used Excel commands. To choose a button, simply click it with the left mouse button. The face of any button has a graphic representation of its function; for instance, the printing button has a printer on its face.

■ **Sheet tabs** below the worksheet grid enable you to keep your work in collections called **workbooks**. Each workbook contains 16 worksheets by default and can contain a maximum of 255 sheets. Sheet tabs can be given meaningful names. **Sheet tab scrolling buttons** help you move from one sheet to another.

■ The **status bar** is located at the bottom of the Excel window. The left side of the status bar provides a brief description of the active command or task in progress. The right side of the status bar shows the status of important keys, such as the Caps Lock key and the Num Lock key.

FIGURE I-4: Excel worksheet window elements

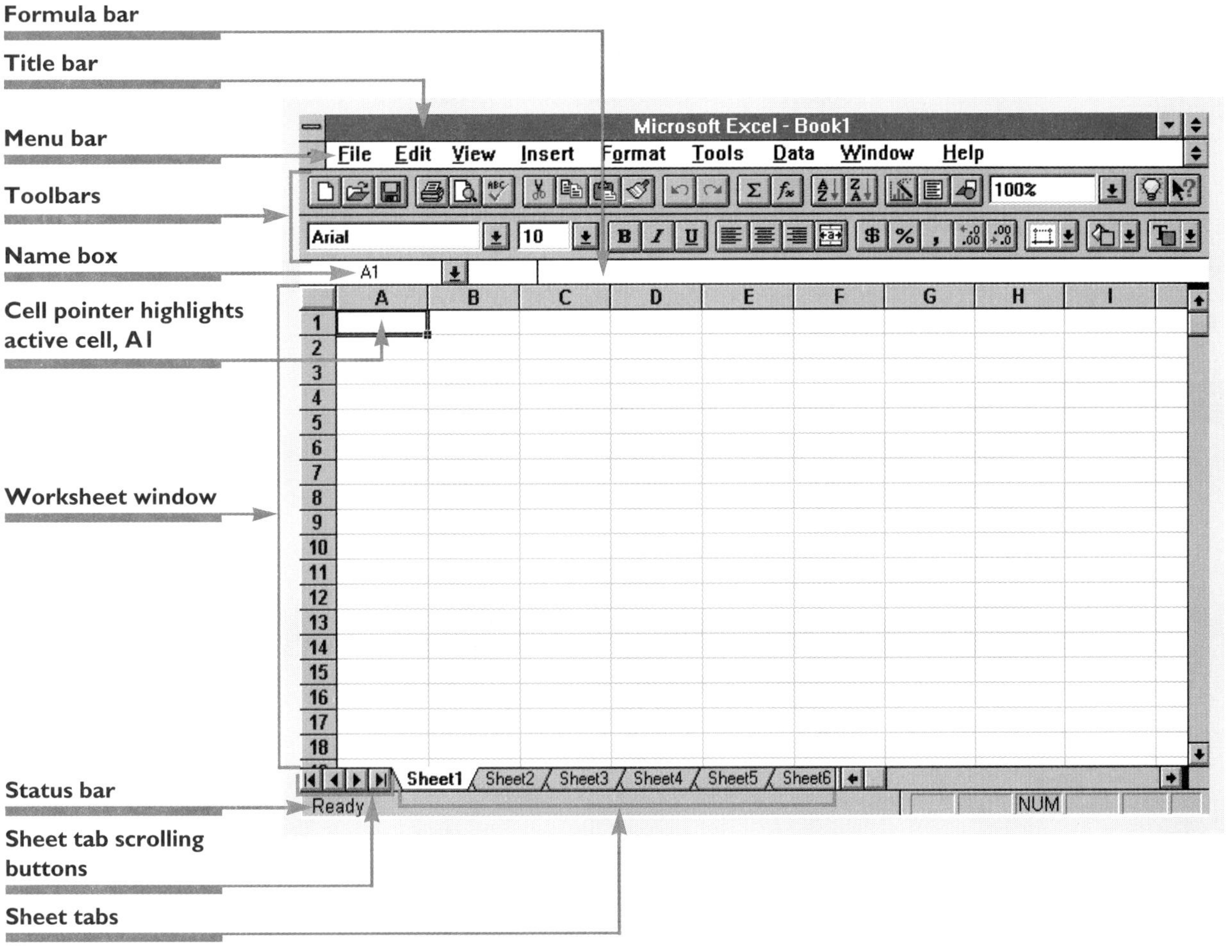

Formula bar

Title bar

Menu bar

Toolbars

Name box

Cell pointer highlights
active cell, AI

Worksheet window

Status bar

Sheet tab scrolling
buttons

Sheet tabs

TROUBLE?

If your worksheet
does not fill the
screen as shown in
Figure 1-4, click the
Maximize button in
the worksheet
window.■

Working with Excel menus and dialog boxes

Like many other Windows applications, Excel provides many commands on its menu bar that you can use to create and format a worksheet. When you choose a menu command that is followed by an ellipsis (...), a dialog box opens. A **dialog box** is a window in which you can specify the options you want for the command. ▶ Evan uses the Format Cells dialog box to enter and format the title for his budget worksheet.

1   Click cell **AI** to make it the active cell
The cell pointer surrounds A1, and A1 appears in the name box.

2   Type **Budget** then press **[Enter]**
The word "Budget" appears in cell A1, aligned on the left side of the cell. To center this text in the cell, you will use a command from the Format menu.

3   Click cell **AI** then click **Format** on the menu bar
The Format menu opens, displaying a list of commands relating to the appearance of the worksheet. See Figure 1-5. You also could have pressed [Alt][O] to open the Format menu. See the related topic "Using keyboard shortcuts" for more information. Notice that a description of the highlighted menu command displays in the status line. The Cells command has an ellipsis after it, which means that a dialog box will display when Evan chooses this command.

4   Click **Cells**
The Format Cells dialog box opens. See Figure 1-6. Many dialog boxes in Excel have tabs like the workbook tabs. The **tabs** separate the various formatting options for the selected command into sub-dialog boxes. The last tab used appears on top. Your screen might display a different tab than the one shown in Figure 1-6.

5   Click the **Alignment tab**
The Alignment tab moves to the front of the dialog box, providing options for changing the alignment of the text in the active cell. Notice the check box next to the Wrap Text option. **Check boxes** toggle an option on or off.

6   In the Horizontal section, click the **round circle** next to the word "Center"
The round circle is called a **radio button**. Radio buttons display when only one option can be chosen in a section of a dialog box.

7   Click **OK** or press **[Enter]**
If a command button in a dialog box has a dark border around it, you can press [Enter] to choose that button. The dialog box closes and the word "Budget" is centered in cell A1.

FIGURE 1-5: Format menu

Ellipsis (...) indicates a dialog box will open

Format menu

Left-aligned text

Description of highlighted menu command

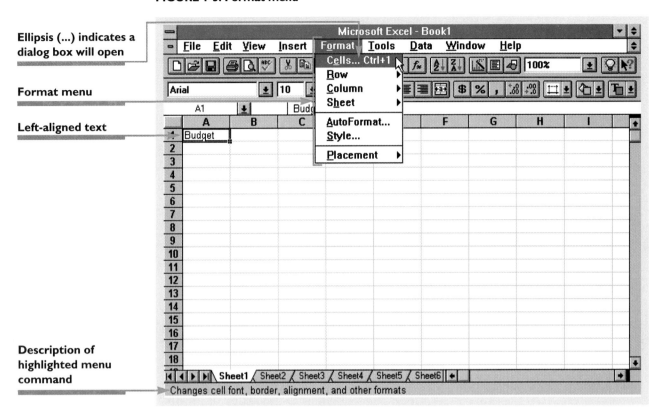

FIGURE 1-6: Format Cells dialog box

Dialog box title bar

Current selection

Dialog box tabs

Dark border means you can press [Enter] to choose command

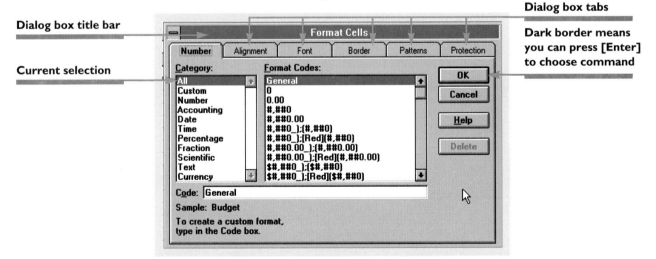

Using keyboard shortcuts

Pointer-movement keys can be used to make choices within a dialog box or menu. To choose a menu from the keyboard, press [Alt] and the underlined letter in the menu you want to select. To choose a command from a menu, press [↑] or [↓], then press [Enter] or press the underlined letter of the command you want to select. To open a new menu, press [→] or [←]. To move within a dialog box, press the underlined letter of the command you want to execute.

QUICK **TIP**

To close a menu without choosing a command, click anywhere outside the menu, or press [Esc].■

Working with buttons

Buttons give you easy access to a variety of commonly used Excel commands. Clicking a button to execute a command is faster than using the menu. Buttons are organized in **toolbars**. The Standard and Formatting toolbars, which appear below the menu bar, are the default toolbars, as shown in Figure 1-7. In addition to these toolbars, Excel provides toolbars that contain buttons for specific purposes such as charting; these will be discussed in future units. You can also customize the toolbars so they contain the buttons for the commands you use most often or reposition them on the screen. See the related topic "Repositioning toolbars" for more information. See Table 1-2 for a description of most frequently used buttons. ▶ Evan uses the Bold button to format his worksheet title, then explores some of the other buttons.

1   Move the mouse pointer over the Bold button 🅱 on the Formatting toolbar, *but do not click the mouse button*
When you move the pointer over a button, the ToolTip associated with that button appears. The **ToolTip** displays the name of the button, and a description of the button appears in the status bar. See Figure 1-8.

2   Click cell **A1** to make it the active cell, then click 🅱
The word Budget becomes bold. The Bold button is a **toggle button**, which means that if you clicked the Bold button again, you would remove the bold formatting. Notice that the Center and Bold buttons appear "depressed," indicating that the cell contents are centered and bold.

3   Move the mouse pointer over the other buttons in the Standard and Formatting toolbars to display the names of these buttons
Notice how much can be accomplished using buttons.

TABLE 1-2:
Frequently used buttons

ICON	NAME	DESCRIPTION
📂	Open	Opens a file
💾	Save	Saves a file
🖨	Print	Opens the Print dialog box
🔍	Print Preview	Shows the worksheet as it will appear when it is printed
✓	Spelling	Checks the spelling in the current workbook
✂	Cut	Cuts the selected range to the Clipboard
📋	Copy	Copies the selected range to the Clipboard
📋	Paste	Pastes Clipboard contents into the current workbook at the cell pointer
🅱	Bold	Adds/removes bold formatting

FIGURE 1-7: Standard and Formatting toolbars

Standard toolbar

Formatting toolbar

FIGURE 1-8: Bold ToolTip

Text centered

ToolTip

Center button depressed to indicate it is activated

Description of selected button

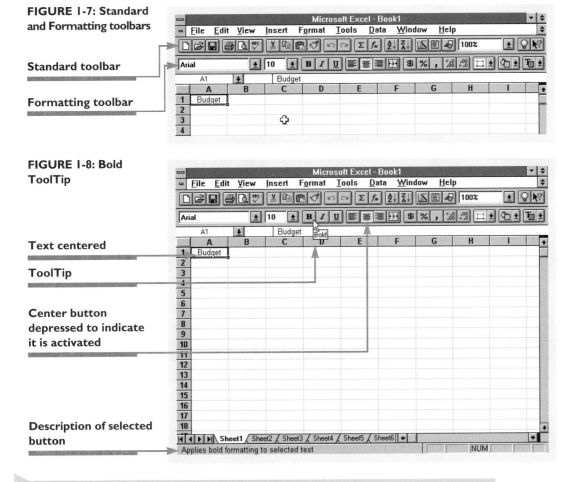

Repositioning toolbars

To allow you to make the best use of your work area, toolbars can be moved and resized. Each toolbar can be positioned along the top of the window, as shown in Figure 1-7, or it can "float" within its own window. To change a toolbar's location, click and hold the pointer in the gray area around the edge of the toolbar, then drag the toolbar away from its current location. To resize a floating toolbar, position the pointer over the edge of the toolbar window until it becomes ⟨↔⟩, then drag the edge until the window is the size you want. In Figure 1-9, the Standard toolbar is floating. Compare Figure 1-9 with Figure 1-8.

Formatting toolbar

Floating toolbar

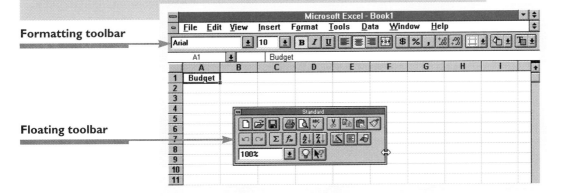

FIGURE 1-9: Standard toolbar floating

Getting Help

Excel features an extensive on-line Help system that gives you immediate access to definitions, explanations, and useful tips. Help information appears in a separate window that you can resize and refer to as you work. ▶ Evan decides to use Excel's on-line Help to learn more about toolbars.

1 Click **Help** on the menu bar, then click **Search for Help on**
The Search dialog box opens. See Figure 1-10. In this dialog box, you can type a specific topic or feature and view the entries that provide more information.

2 In the search text box, type **too**
Notice as you type each character, the alphabetically arranged topics scroll in the search topics list below the text box. After you type the second o, "toolbars" appears in the list.

3 Click **toolbars** then click **Show Topics**
A list of related topics displays in the box at the bottom of the dialog box.

4 Scroll down the show topics list until you see the topic "Moving and resizing toolbars," click to select it, then click **Go To**
Two windows open: Help and How To. If the How To window appears under the Help window, click within its border to make the How To window active. See Figure 1-11. Depending on the type and size of your monitor, the two windows might appear on different sides of the screen. The Help window contains buttons that will lead you through different sets of instructions for Excel. Help buttons appearing under the Help menu bar are described in Table 1-3. The How To window displays information about moving and resizing toolbars, the topic you selected. You can click the words with the green dotted underline (or black dotted underline, depending on your monitor) to open a pop-up window with more information about that topic.

5 Move the pointer to the dotted-underline text **floating toolbar** until the pointer changes to ⅏, then click
Depending on your monitor, this text could have a black dotted underline or a green dotted underline. A pop-up window containing a definition of a floating toolbar opens.

6 After reading the information, click anywhere outside the pop-up window or press **[Esc]** to close the pop-up window
Clicking the Overview button will display general information about customizing toolbars in the Help window. You can use the Example and Practice button to see examples of the topic you've selected or to practice performing a task.

7 Click the **Overview button**
Evan reads this information and then decides to close the Help window.

8 Click **File** on the Help window menu bar, then click **Exit**
The Help window closes and you return to your worksheet.

FIGURE 1-10: Search dialog box

Search text box

Search topics list

Show topics list

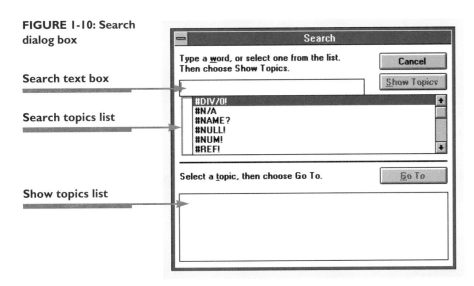

FIGURE 1-11: Help and How To windows

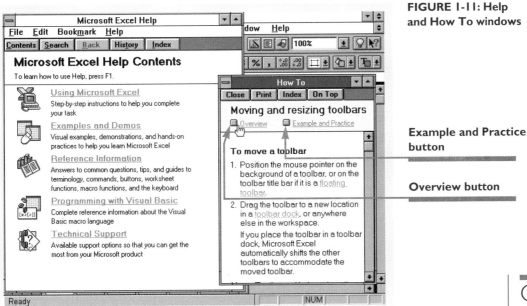

Example and Practice button

Overview button

TABLE 1-3: The Help buttons

BUTTON	DESCRIPTION
Contents	Displays Help topic categories
Search	Displays search dialog box in which you can search for a specific topic
Back	Returns you to the previous topic
History	Displays a list of Help topics to which you have recently referred
Index	Displays an alphabetical listing of topics

QUICK **TIP**

If you need help while you are working on a particular topic, click the Help button ▨ on the Standard toolbar. The mouse pointer changes to **?**. Point to a part of the worksheet or a command on a menu, and then click. Excel's Help system displays context-sensitive information about your current location.■

Moving around the worksheet

With over a billion cells available to you, it's important to know how to move around, or **navigate**, the worksheet. If you want to move up, down, or over one or two cells, you can simply press the pointer-movement keys ([↑] [↓] [←] [→]). To move longer distances within the worksheet window, you might prefer to use the mouse and click the desired cell address. If the desired cell address is not visible within the worksheet window, you can use the scroll bars or the Go To command to move the location into view. Table 1-4 lists helpful techniques for moving around the worksheet. Evan uses a combination of methods to practice navigating the worksheet.

I   **Click cell I18**
The cell pointer highlights cell I18 in the lower-right corner of your worksheet window.

2   **Press [→]**
The cell pointer moves over one cell to J18, moving the entire worksheet over one column. Notice that cell A1, which contains the word "Budget," is no longer visible in the worksheet window.

3   **On the vertical scroll bar, click the down arrow once**
The worksheet window scrolls down one row, so that row 1 scrolls off the top of the window. You can move a window's contents one row or column at a time by clicking on the vertical or horizontal scroll bar arrows. You can move a screenful at a time by clicking on either side of a scroll box.

4   **Click to the right of the horizontal scroll box**
Columns K through S should appear in your worksheet window. If you need to travel a great distance across a worksheet, you can use the Go To command.

5   **Click Edit on the menu bar, then click Go To**
The Go To dialog box opens. See Figure 1-12. You could also press [F5] to display the Go To dialog box.

6   **Type Z1000 in the Reference text box, then click OK**
The cell pointer highlights cell Z1000 in the lower-right corner of the worksheet window. You could use the Go To command or the scroll bars to move the cell pointer back to the beginning of the worksheet, but there is a faster way to move the cell pointer directly to cell A1.

7   **Press [Ctrl][Home]**
The cell pointer highlights cell A1.

FIGURE 1-12: Go To dialog box

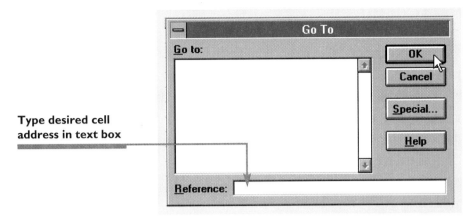

Type desired cell address in text box

TABLE 1-4: Worksheet navigation techniques

TO MOVE	DO THIS
Up one row	Press [↑]
Down one row	Press [↓]
Left one cell	Press [←]
Right one cell	Press [→]
Up one screenful	Press [PgUp]
Down one screenful	Press [PgDn]
Left one screenful	Press [Alt][PgUp]
Right one screenful	Press [Alt][PgDn]
Left one column	Click the left arrow on the horizontal scroll bar
Right one column	Click the right arrow on the horizontal scroll bar
Cell A1	Press [Ctrl][Home]
Column A in current row	Press [Home]
Last active column in current row	Press [End]

Naming a sheet

Each workbook initially contains 16 worksheets. When the workbook is first open, the first worksheet is the active sheet. To move from sheet to sheet, click the desired sheet tab located at the bottom of the worksheet window. Sheet tab scrolling buttons, located to the left of the sheet tabs, allow rapid movement among the sheets. To make it easier to identify the sheets in a workbook, you can name each sheet. The name appears on the sheet tab. For instance, sheets within a single workbook could be named for individual sales people to better track performance goals.

▶ Evan practices moving from sheet to sheet and decides to name two sheets in his workbook.

1   Click the Sheet2 tab
Sheet2 becomes active. Its tab moves to the front, and the tab for Sheet1 moves to the background. The word "Budget" disappears from view because it is in cell A1 of Sheet1.

2   Click the Sheet5 tab
Sheet5 becomes active. Now Evan will rename Sheet1 so it has a name that he can easily remember.

3   Double-click the Sheet1 tab
The Rename Sheet dialog box opens with the default sheet name (Sheet1) selected in the Name text box. You could also click Format in the menu bar, click Sheet, then click Rename to display the Rename Sheet dialog box.

4   Type Qtrly Budget in the Name text box
See Figure 1-13. The new name automatically replaced the default name in the Name text box. Worksheet names can have up to 31 characters, including spaces and punctuation.

5   Click OK
Notice that the tab of the first sheet says "Qtrly Budget." See Figure 1-14.

6   Double-click Sheet2 then rename this sheet Additional Info
You can also rearrange sheets if necessary. See the related topic "Moving sheets" for additional information.

FIGURE 1-13: Rename Sheet dialog box

Type new sheet name here ⟶

FIGURE 1-14: Renamed sheet in workbook

Sheet tab scrolling buttons

Sheet1 renamed

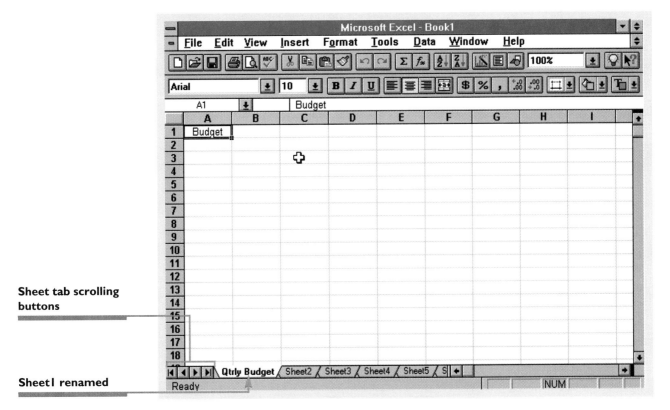

Moving sheets

You can easily rearrange worksheets in a workbook. To move a sheet, position the mouse pointer on the sheet tab, click and hold the left mouse button, then drag the sheet tab to its new location. A small arrow and an icon of a document just above the sheet tabs indicates the new location of the worksheet, as shown in Figure 1-15.

New location indicator

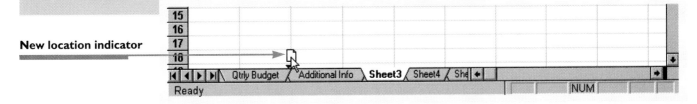

FIGURE 1-15: Moving Sheet3 after Qtrly Budget sheet

Closing a workbook and exiting Excel

When you have finished working on a workbook, you need to save the file and close it. To close a file, click Close on the File menu. When you have completed all your work in Excel, you need to exit the application. To exit Excel, click Exit on the File menu. For a comparison of the Close and Exit commands, refer to Table 1-5. ▶ Evan needs to gather more information before creating his worksheet, so he closes the workbook and then exits Excel.

1   Click **File** on the menu bar
See Figure 1-16.

2   Click **Close**
You could also double-click the workbook control menu box instead of choosing File Close. A dialog box opens, asking if you want to save changes in "Book1" before closing. See Figure 1-17. Because he was only practicing, Evan does not want to save the workbook.

3   Click **No**
Excel closes the workbook and displays a blank worksheet window. Notice that the menu bar contains only the File and Help menu choices.

4   Click **File** then click **Exit**
You could also double-click the application control menu box to exit the application. Excel closes and computer memory is freed up for other computing tasks.

TABLE I-5: Excel's Close and Exit commands

CLOSING A FILE	EXITING EXCEL
Puts away a workbook file	Puts away all workbook files
Leaves Excel running if you choose to open another file	Returns you to the Program Manager where you can choose to run another application

FIGURE 1-16: Closing a workbook using the File menu

Application control menu box

Workbook control menu box

Close command

Exit command

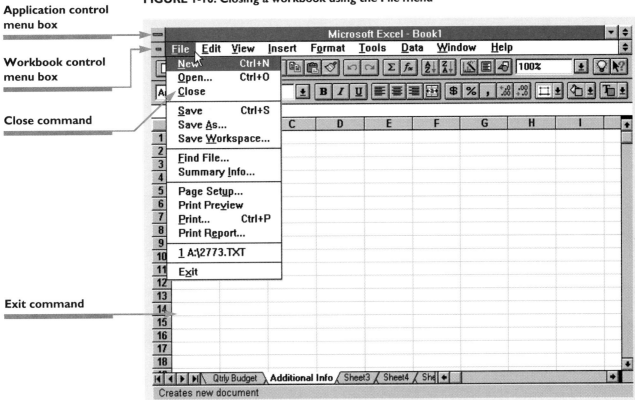

FIGURE 1-17: Microsoft Excel save changes dialog box

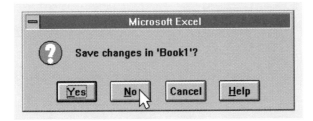

QUICK **TIP**

To exit Excel and close several files at once, choose Exit from the File menu. Excel will prompt you to save changes to each workbook before exiting.∎

CONCEPTSREVIEW

Label each of the elements of the Excel worksheet window shown in Figure 1-18.

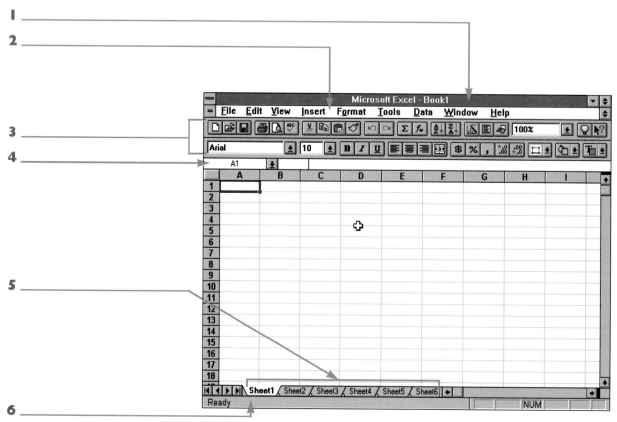

FIGURE 1-18

Match each of the terms with the statement that describes its function.

7 Area that contains a grid of columns and rows

8 The intersection of a column and row

9 Graphic symbol that depicts a task or function

10 Collection of worksheets

11 Rectangle that indicates the cell you are currently working in

12 Displays the active cell address

a. Cell pointer

b. Button

c. Worksheet window

d. Name box

e. Cell

f. Workbook

Select the best answer from the list of choices.

13 An electronic spreadsheet can perform all of the following tasks, EXCEPT:

a. Display information visually

b. Calculate data accurately

c. Plan worksheet objectives

d. Recalculate updated information

14 You can move a screen at a time all of the following ways, EXCEPT:

a. Press [PgUp]

b. Press [Alt][PgDn]

c. Press [Alt][PgUp]

d. Press [↑]

15 Which key(s) do you press to move quickly to cell A1?

   a. [Ctrl][Home]

   b. [Alt]

   c. [Esc][Home]

   d. [Enter]

16 A menu command that is followed by an ellipsis means

   a. The command is not currently available

   b. Clicking the command will display a dialog box

   c. Clicking the command will display a submenu

   d. The command has no keyboard shortcut

17 You can get Excel Help any of the following ways, EXCEPT:

   a. Clicking Help on the menu bar

   b. Pressing [F1]

   c. Clicking the Help button ▣ on the Standard toolbar

   d. Minimizing the application window

18 Which key(s) do you press to move the active cell to the right one column?

   a. [Enter]

   b. [Right Arrow]

   c. [Esc]

   d. [Alt][R]

19 How do you open the Rename Sheet dialog box?

   a. Double-click any sheet tab scrolling button

   b. Click the name box list arrow with the right mouse button

   c. Click the Name Sheet Tab button

   d. Double-click the sheet tab

20 Which key(s) move the cell pointer quickly to the last active column in the current row?

   a. [Ctrl][End]

   b. [Alt]

   c. [End]

   d. [Enter]

21 Which of the following statements about buttons is *NOT* true?

   a. You choose a button by clicking it.

   b. You can move a button by dragging it.

   c. A ToolTip, which describes the button, displays when you position the mouse pointer over the button.

   d. Buttons appear depressed when selected.

APPLICATIONS
REVIEW

1 Start Excel and identify the elements in the worksheet window.

   a. Double-click the Microsoft Office group icon in the Program Manager window.

   b. Double-click the Microsoft Excel application icon.

   c. Try to identify as many elements in the Excel worksheet window as you can without referring to the unit material.

2 Explore Excel menus.

   a. Click Edit on the menu bar. Notice that a description of the highlighted Undo command displays in the status bar.

   b. Drag through the commands on the Edit menu so that you can review the brief descriptions in the status bar. Press [Esc] if necessary.

   c. Click Format on the menu bar.

   d. Move through the commands using [↓], and review the descriptions in the status bar.

   e. Click Cells on the Format menu to display the Format Cells dialog box. Click each of the tabs and review the options for each tab. Press [Esc] or click cancel.

   f. Review other commands on the Excel menu bar in the same fashion.

3 Explore buttons.

   a. Position the mouse pointer over each button on the Standard and Formatting toolbars.

   b. Write down each button's function.

   c. Start a list of buttons that duplicate menu commands. Add to this list as you come across more buttons that duplicate menu commands.

4 Explore Excel Help.

   a. Click Help on the menu bar.

   b. Click Search for Help on. The Search dialog box displays.

   c. Identify all of the buttons that appear in the Search dialog box.

   d. Click the down scroll arrow on the search topics list box to view available topics.

   e. Select a topic from the list box, then click Show Topics.

   f. Select a topic to read, then click Go To.

   g. Click File on the Help menu bar, then click Exit.

5 Move around the worksheet.

a. Press [Ctrl][Home] to move the cell pointer to cell A1.

b. Press [→] once to move the cell pointer right one column.

c. Press [↓] twice to move the cell pointer down two rows to cell B3.

d. Click the right arrow on the horizontal scroll bar to move the screen to the right by one column.

e. Click the left arrow on the horizontal scroll bar to move the screen back to its original column display.

6 Name a sheet.

a. Double-click the Sheet3 tab.

b. Type "March" in the Rename Sheet dialog box, then click OK.

c. Click the Sheet4 tab.

d. Click the Sheet2 tab.

e. Double-click the Sheet1 tab.

f. Type "January" in the Rename Sheet dialog box, then click OK.

7 Close the workbook and exit Excel.

a. Click File on the menu bar, then click Close.

b. Click No when asked if you want to save the worksheet.

c. If necessary, close any other worksheets you might have opened.

d. Click File on the menu bar, then click Exit.

INDEPENDENT
CHALLENGE I

Excel's on-line Help provides definitions, explanations, procedures, and other helpful information. It also provides examples and demonstrations to show you how Excel features work. Topics include elements such as the active cell, status bar, buttons, and dialog boxes, as well as detailed information about Excel commands and options. To explore Help, click Examples and Demos from the Help menu, then read all the information on the "Using Toolbars" and "Selecting Cells, Choosing Commands" topics. Use the Search for Help on command to find information about dialog boxes, the active cell, and the status bar. Return to your workbook when you are finished reading about these Excel features.

INDEPENDENT
CHALLENGE 2

Spreadsheet software has many uses that can affect the way work is done. Some examples of how Excel can be used are discussed in the beginning of this unit. Use your own personal or business experiences to come up with five examples of how Excel could be used in a business setting.

To complete this independent challenge:

1 Think of five business tasks that you could complete more efficiently using an Excel worksheet.

2 Sketch a sample of each worksheet. See Figure 1-19, which is an example of a payroll worksheet.

3 Submit your sketches.

Employee Names	Hours Worked	Hourly Wage	Gross Pay	
Janet Bryce			→	Gross pay=
Anthony Krups			→	Hours worked
Grant Miller			→	times
Barbara Salazar			→	Hourly wage
Total	↓	↓	↓	

FIGURE I-19

UNIT 2

OBJECTIVES

- ▶ Plan and design a worksheet
- ▶ Enter labels
- ▶ Enter values
- ▶ Edit cell entries
- ▶ Work with ranges
- ▶ Enter formulas
- ▶ Use Excel functions
- ▶ Save a workbook
- ▶ Preview and print a worksheet

Creating
A WORKSHEET

Now that you are familiar with Excel menus, dialog boxes, tools, and on-line Help system and you know how to navigate within an Excel work-book, you are ready to plan and build your own worksheets. When you build a worksheet, you enter text, values, and formulas into worksheet cells. Once you create a worksheet, you can save the workbook containing the worksheet and print it. Helping managers plan for the future is one of the many ways Excel is useful for businesses. ▶ Evan Brillstein has received a request from the Marketing Department for a forecast of this year's anticipated summer tour business. Marketing hopes that the tour business will increase 20% over last year's figures. ▶

Planning and designing a worksheet

Before you start entering data into a worksheet, you need to know the purpose and approximate layout of the worksheet. Evan wants to forecast Nomad's 1995 summer tour sales. The sales goal, identified by the Marketing Department, for the summer of 1995 is to increase the 1994 summer sales totals by 20%. ▶ Using Figure 2-1 and the planning guidelines below, follow Evan as he plans his worksheet.

■ **Determine the purpose of the worksheet and give it a meaningful title.**
Evan needs to forecast summer tour sales for 1995. Evan titles the worksheet "1995 Summer Tour Sales Forecast."

■ **Determine your worksheet's desired results, sometimes called output.**
Evan needs to determine what the 1995 sales totals will be if sales increase by 20% over the 1994 sales totals.

■ **Collect all the information, sometimes called input, that will produce the results you want to see.**
Evan gathers together the sales data for the 1994 summer tour season. The season ran from June through August. The types of tours sold in these months included Bike, Raft, Horse, and Bus.

■ **Determine the calculations, or formulas, necessary to achieve the desired results.**
First, Evan needs to total the number of tours sold for each month of the 1994 summer season. Then he needs to add these totals together to determine the grand total of summer tour sales. Finally, the 1994 monthly totals and grand total must be multiplied by 1.2 to calculate a 20% increase for the 1995 summer tour season.

■ **Sketch on paper how you want the worksheet to look; that is, identify where the labels and values will go. Labels are text entries that describe and help you understand the data in a worksheet. Values are the numbers used in calculations.**
Evan decides to put tour types in rows and the months in columns. He enters the tour sales data in his sketch and indicates where the monthly sales totals and the grand total should go. Below the totals, he writes out the formula for determining a 20% increase in sales for 1995. Evan's sketch of his worksheet is shown in Figure 2-1.

FIGURE 2-1: Worksheet sketch showing labels, values, and calculations

1995 Summer Tours Sales Forecast

	June	July	August	Totals
Bike	14	10	6	3 month total
Raft	7	8	12	
Horse	12	7	6	
Bus	1	2	9	
				Grand Total
Totals	June Total	July Total	August Total	for 1994
1995 Sales	Total x 1.2			

Entering labels

Labels are used to identify the data in the rows and columns of a worksheet. They are also used to make your worksheet readable and understandable. For these reasons, you should enter all labels in your worksheet first. Labels can contain text and numerical information not used in calculations such as dates, times, or address numbers. Labels are left-aligned by default. ▶ Using his sketch as a guide, Evan begins building his worksheet by entering the labels.

1 **Start Excel and make sure you have an empty workbook in the Excel worksheet window**
   If you need help starting Excel, refer to the lesson "Starting Excel 5.0 for Windows" in Unit 1.

2 **Click cell B4 to make it the active cell**
   Notice that the cell address B4 appears in the name box. Now Evan enters the worksheet title.

3 **Type 1995 Summer Tours Sales Forecast, as shown in Figure 2-2, then click the Enter button ▣ on the formula bar**
   You must click ▣ or use one of the other methods listed in Table 2-1 to confirm your entry. Notice that the title does not fit in cell B4 and spreads across several columns. If a label does not fit in a cell, Excel displays the remaining characters in the next cell as long as it is empty. Otherwise, the label is truncated, or cut off. The contents of B4, the active cell, displays in the formula bar. When a cell contains both text and numbers, Excel recognizes the entry as a label. If you want to enter a number as a label, you would type an apostrophe (') before the first number.

4 **Click cell A6, type Bike, then press [Enter] to complete the entry and move the cell pointer to cell A7; type Raft in cell A7, then press [Enter]; type Horse in cell A8, then press [Enter]; then type Bus in cell A9, then press [Enter]**
   Now Evan enters the labels for the rows containing the totals and the 1995 sales forecast.

5 **Click cell A11, type Total, then press [Enter]; click cell A13, type 1995 Sales, then press [Enter]**
   Next he enters the labels for the summer months.

6 **Click cell B5, type June, then click ▣; click cell C5, type July, then click ▣; click cell D5, type August, then click ▣**

7 **Click cell E5, type Total, then click ▣**
   All the labels for Evan's worksheet are now entered. See Figure 2-3.

FIGURE 2-2: Worksheet with title entered

Enter button

Formula bar

Title spreads across
columns

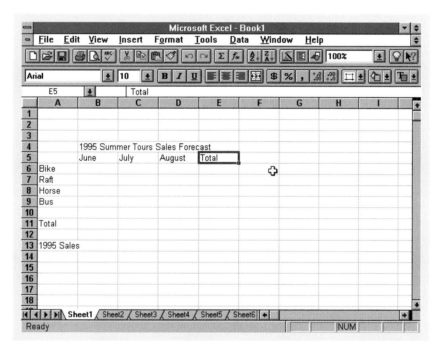

FIGURE 2-3: Worksheet with labels entered

TABLE 2-1: Confirming cell entries

ACTION	CONFIRMS ENTRY THEN
Click ▨	Cell pointer stays in current cell
Press [Enter]	Moves the cell pointer one row down
Press [Shift][Enter]	Moves the cell pointer one row up
Press [Tab]	Moves the cell pointer one column to the right
Press [Shift][Tab]	Moves the cell pointer one column to the left
Click in another cell	Moves the cell pointer to the cell that is clicked

TROUBLE?

If you notice a mistake
in a cell entry after it
has been confirmed,
select the cell you want
to edit and press [F2].
Use [Backspace] and
[Delete] to make any
corrections, then click
the Enter button ▨ or
press [Enter] to confirm
the corrected entry.■

Entering values

Values, which include numbers, formulas, and functions, are used in calculations. Excel recognizes an entry as a value when it is a number or begins with one of these symbols: +, -, =, @, #, or $. All values are right-aligned by default.
► Evan enters the sales data from the 1994 summer season into his worksheet.

1   Click cell **B6**, type **14**, then press **[Enter]**; type **7** in cell B7, then press **[Enter]**; type **12** in cell B8, then press **[Enter]**; type **1** in cell B9, then press **[Enter]**

   All the tour sales for the month of June are now entered. Now Evan enters the sales for the month of July.

2   Click cell **C6**, type **10**, then press **[Enter]**; type **8** in cell C7, then press **[Enter]**; type **7** in cell C8, then press **[Enter]**; type **2** in cell C9, then press **[Enter]**

   Next he enters the tour sales for August.

3   Click cell **D6**, type **6**, then press **[Enter]**; type **12** in cell D7, then press **[Enter]**; type **6** in cell D8, then press **[Enter]**; type **9** in cell D9, then press **[Enter]**

   Evan has entered all the labels and data he needs for his worksheet. Compare your worksheet to Figure 2-4.

FIGURE 2-4 Worksheet with labels and values entered

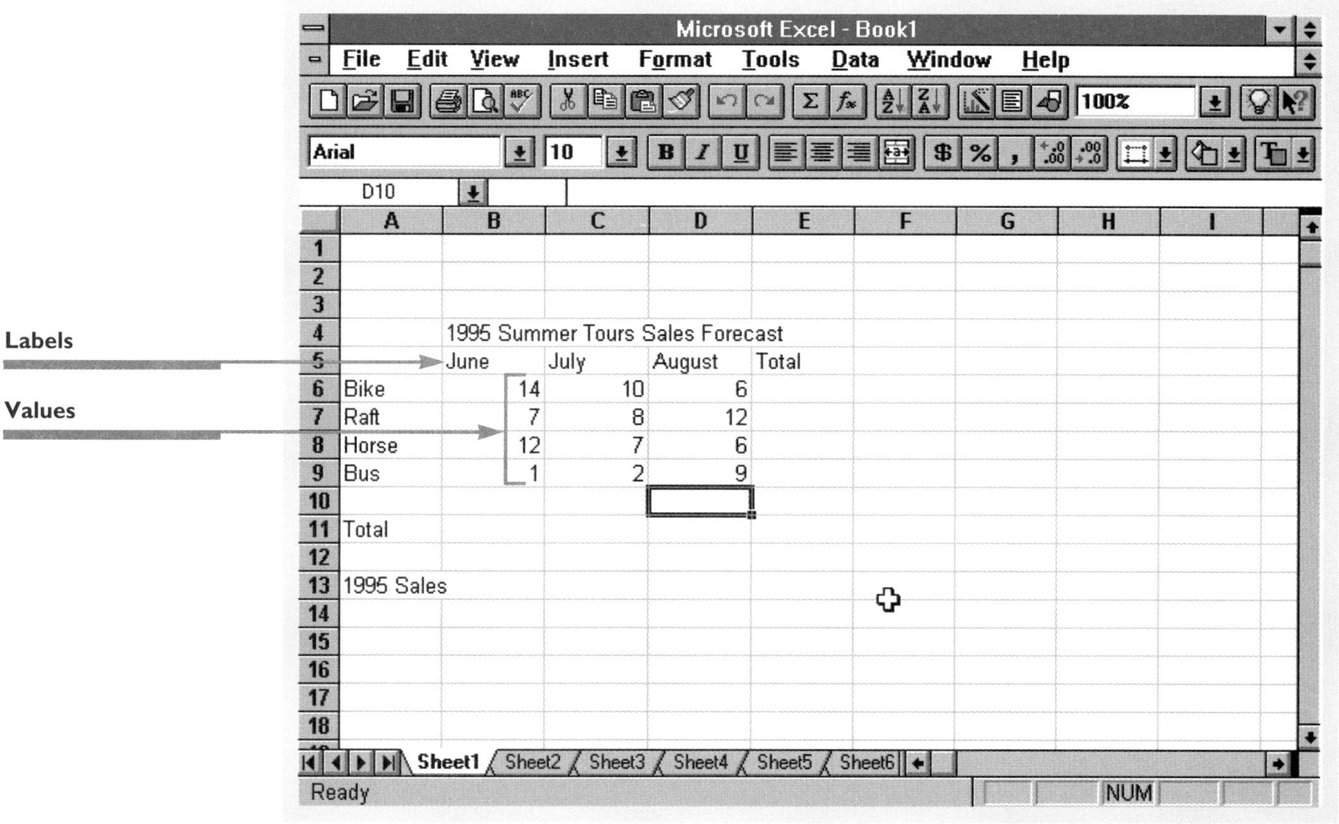

Labels

Values

	A	B	C	D	E	F	G	H	I
1									
2									
3									
4		1995 Summer Tours Sales Forecast							
5		June	July	August	Total				
6	Bike	14	10	6					
7	Raft	7	8	12					
8	Horse	12	7	6					
9	Bus	1	2	9					
10									
11	Total								
12									
13	1995 Sales								
14									
15									
16									
17									
18									

Microsoft Excel - Book1

File   Edit   View   Insert   Format   Tools   Data   Window   Help

Arial   10   B I U

D10

Sheet1 / Sheet2 / Sheet3 / Sheet4 / Sheet5 / Sheet6

Ready   NUM

QUICK **TIP**

To enter a number, such as the year 1994, as a label so it will not be included in a calculation, type an apostrophe (') before the number. ■

Editing cell entries

You can change the contents of any cells at any time. To edit the contents of a cell, you first select the cell you want to edit, then click the formula bar, double-click the selected cell, or press [F2]. This puts Excel into Edit mode. To make sure you are in Edit mode, check the mode indicator on the far left of the status bar. Refer to Table 2-2 for more information on the mode indicator. ▶ After checking his worksheet, Evan notices that he entered the wrong value for the June bus tours and forgot to include the canoe tours. He fixes the bus tours figure, and he decides to add the canoe sales data to the raft sales figures.

I Click cell **B9**

This cell contains June bus tours, which Evan needs to change to 2.

2 Click anywhere in the formula bar

Excel goes into Edit mode, and the mode indicator displays "Edit." A blinking vertical line, called the **insertion point**, appears in the formula bar, and if you move the mouse pointer to the formula bar, the pointer changes to Ⅰ. See Figure 2-5.

3 Press **[Backspace]**, type **2**, then press **[Enter]** or click the **Enter button** ⬜ on the formula bar

Evan now needs to add "/Canoe" to the Raft label.

4 Click cell **A7** then press **[F2]**

Excel is in Edit mode again, but the insertion point is in the cell.

5 Type **/Canoe** then press **[Enter]**

The label changes to Raft/Canoe, which is a little too long to fit in the cell. Don't worry about this. You will learn how to change the width of a column later.

6 Double-click cell **B7**

Double-clicking a cell also puts Excel into Edit mode with the insertion point in the cell.

7 Press **[Delete]** then type **9**

See Figure 2-6.

8 Click ⬜ to confirm the entry

You can also cancel the entry if you notice a mistake. See the related topic "Using the Cancel button" for more information.

TABLE 2-2: Understanding the mode indicator

MODE	DESCRIPTION
Edit	You are editing a cell entry.
Enter	You are entering data.
Error	You have made an entry Excel cannot understand; click the Help tool 📭 on the Standard toolbar or click OK.
Point	You have specified a range without a formula.
Ready	Excel is ready for you to enter data or choose a command.
Wait	Excel is completing a task.

FIGURE 2-5: Worksheet in Edit mode

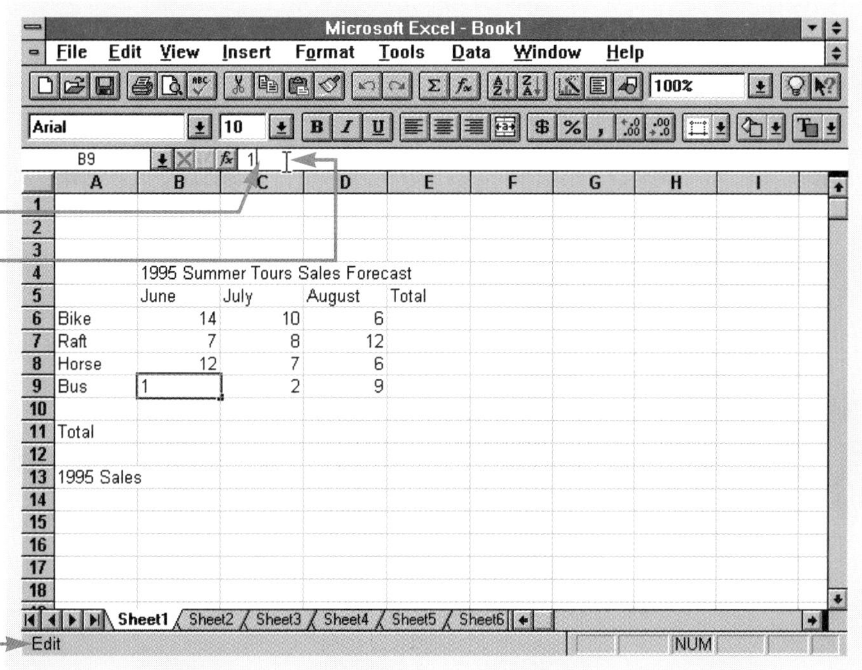

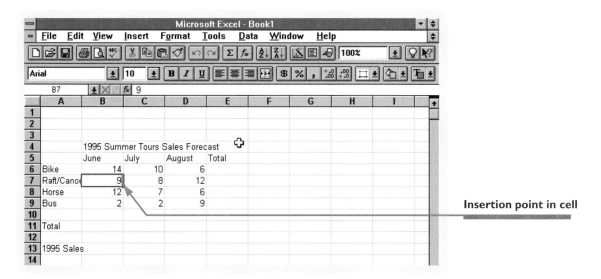

Insertion point in formula bar

Mouse pointer

Edit mode indicator

FIGURE 2-6: Worksheet with edits completed

Insertion point in cell

Using the Cancel button

When you enter data into a cell, the Cancel button ☒ appears immediately to the left of the Enter button ☐ on the formula bar. If you make a mistake entering data or editing a cell entry, you can click the Cancel button instead of confirming the entry. This removes the data entered, and the cell reverts to its original contents.

QUICK **TIP**

If you make a mistake, click the Undo button ⟲ on the Standard toolbar or choose Undo from the Edit menu before doing anything else.■

Working with ranges

Any group of cells (two or more) is called a **range**. To select a range, click the first cell and drag to the last cell you want included in the range. The range address is defined by noting the first and last cells in the range. Figure 2-7 shows a selected range whose address is B6:C9. You can give a meaningful name to a range, and then use the range name in formulas. Named ranges are usually easier to remember than cell addresses and they also help you move around the workbook quickly. See the related topic "Using range names to move around the workbook" for more information. ▶ To make his forecasting worksheet easier to understand, Evan decides to use named ranges in the worksheet.

1 Click cell **B6** then drag to cell **B9** to select the range B6:B9

2 Click the **name box** to select the cell address B6

3 Type **June** then press **[Enter]**
   Now whenever cells B6:B9 are selected, the range name "June" will appear in the name box.

4 Click cell **C6** then drag to cell **C9** to select the range C6:C9; click the **name box**, type **July**, then press **[Enter]**

5 Click cell **D6** then drag to cell **D9** to select the range D6:D9; click the **name box**, type **August**, then press **[Enter]**
   Next, Evan names the four ranges containing the data for each type of tour.

6 Select the range **B6:D6**, click the **name box**, type **Bike**, then press **[Enter]**

7 Name the range B7:D7 **RaftCanoe**, range B8:D8 **Horse**, and range B9:D9 **Bus**
   Note that there is no slash separating the words Raft and Canoe in the range name for the range B7:D7.

8 Click the **name box list arrow** to see the list of range names in this worksheet
   Notice that the named ranges are in alphabetical order. See Figure 2-8.

9 Click anywhere outside the range name list to close it

FIGURE 2-7:
Worksheet showing
selected range of cells

Name box

Selected range

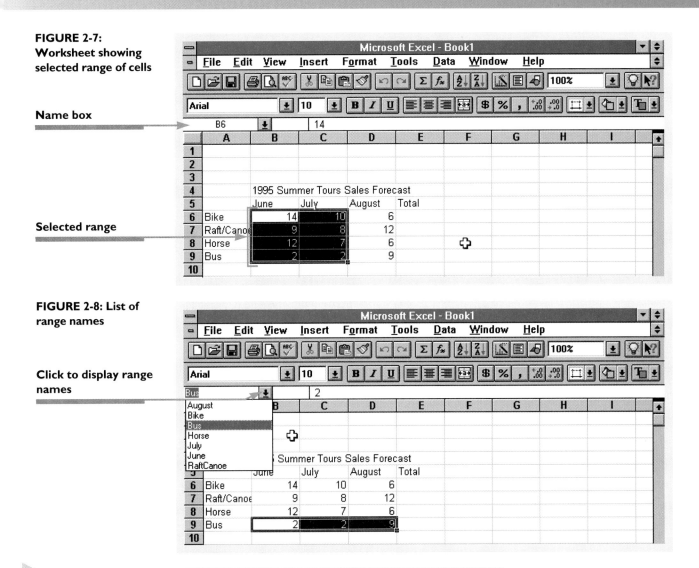

FIGURE 2-8: List of
range names

Click to display range
names

Using range names to move around a workbook

You can use range names to move around a workbook quickly. Click the name box list arrow, then click the name of the range you want to go to, as shown in Figure 2-9. The cell pointer moves immediately to that range in the workbook.

August range selected

Cell pointer moves to
selected range

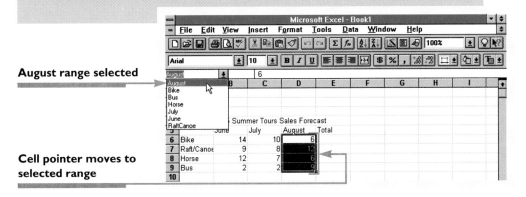

FIGURE 2-9: Moving the cell pointer using range names

TROUBLE?

If you make a mistake selecting and naming a range, click Insert on the menu bar, click Name, then click Define. In the Define Name dialog box, high-light the range name you need to redefine, click Delete, then click Close. Select and name the range again.■

Entering formulas

Formulas are used to perform numeric calculations such as adding, multiplying and averaging. Formulas in an Excel worksheet start with the formula prefix—the equal sign (=). All formulas use **arithmetic operators** to perform calculations. See Table 2-3 for a list of Excel operators. Formulas often contain cell addresses and range names. Using a cell address or range name in a formula is called **cell referencing**. Using cell references keeps your worksheet up-to-date and accurate. If you change a value in a cell, any formula containing that cell reference will be automatically recalculated using the new value. ▶ Evan uses formulas to add the monthly tour totals for June, July, and August.

1 Click cell **B11**
This is the cell where Evan wants to put the calculation that will total the June sales.

2 Type **=** (equal sign)
The equal sign at the beginning of an entry tells Excel that a formula is about to be entered rather than a label or a value. The total June sales is equal to the sum of the values in cells B6, B7, B8, and B9.

3 Type **b6+b7+b8+b9** then click the **Enter button** ▢ on the formula bar
The result of 37 appears in cell B11, and the formula appears in the formula bar. See Figure 2-10. Next, Evan adds the number of tours in July.

4 Click cell **C11**, type **=c6+c7+c8+c9**, then click ▢
The result of 27 appears in C11. Finally, Evan enters the formula to calculate the August tour sales.

5 Click cell **D11**, type **=d6+d7+d8+d9**, then click ▢
The total tour sales for August appears in cell D11. Compare your results with Figure 2-11.

TABLE 2-3: Excel arithmetic operators

OPERATOR	PURPOSE	EXAMPLE
+	Performs addition	=A5+A7
-	Performs subtraction	=A5-10
*	Performs multiplication	=A5*A7
/	Performs division	=A5/A7

FIGURE 2-10: Worksheet showing formula and result

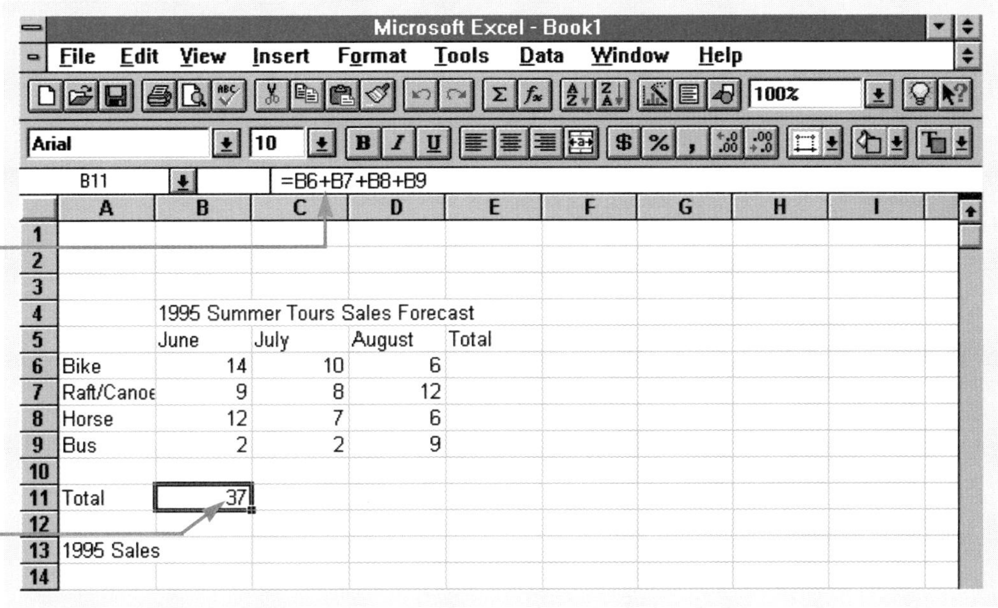

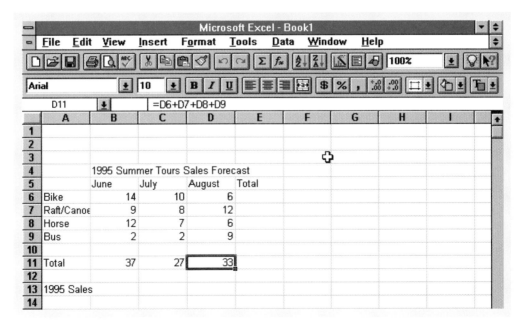

Formula in formula bar

Calculated result in cell

FIGURE 2-11: Worksheet with formulas for monthly totals entered

TROUBLE?

If the formula instead of the result appears in the cell after you click the Enter button ![button], make sure you began the formula with = (equal sign).■

Entering formulas, continued

Formulas can contain more than one arithmetic operator. In these situations, Excel decides which operation to perform first. See the related topic "Order of precedence in Excel formulas" for more information. ▶ Now that Evan has calculated the monthly total tour sales for 1994, he can use these figures to calculate the forecast for 1995. He will use the multiplication symbol, * (the asterisk), to write the formula calculating a 20% increase of 1994 sales. This time he will click the cell address to be included in the formula rather than typing it.

6 Click cell **B13**, type **=**, click cell **B11**, type ***1.2**, then click the **Enter button** 🔲 on the formula bar

To calculate the 20% increase you multiply the total by 1.2. This formula calculates the result of multiplying the total monthly tour sales for June, cell B11, by 1.2. The result of 44.4 appears in cell B13.

Now Evan calculates the 20% increase for July and August.

7 Click cell **C13**, type **=**, click cell **C11**, type ***1.2**, then click 🔲

8 Click cell **D13**, type **=**, click cell **D11**, type ***1.2**, then click 🔲

Compare your results with Figure 2-12.

FIGURE 2-12: Calculated results for 20% increase

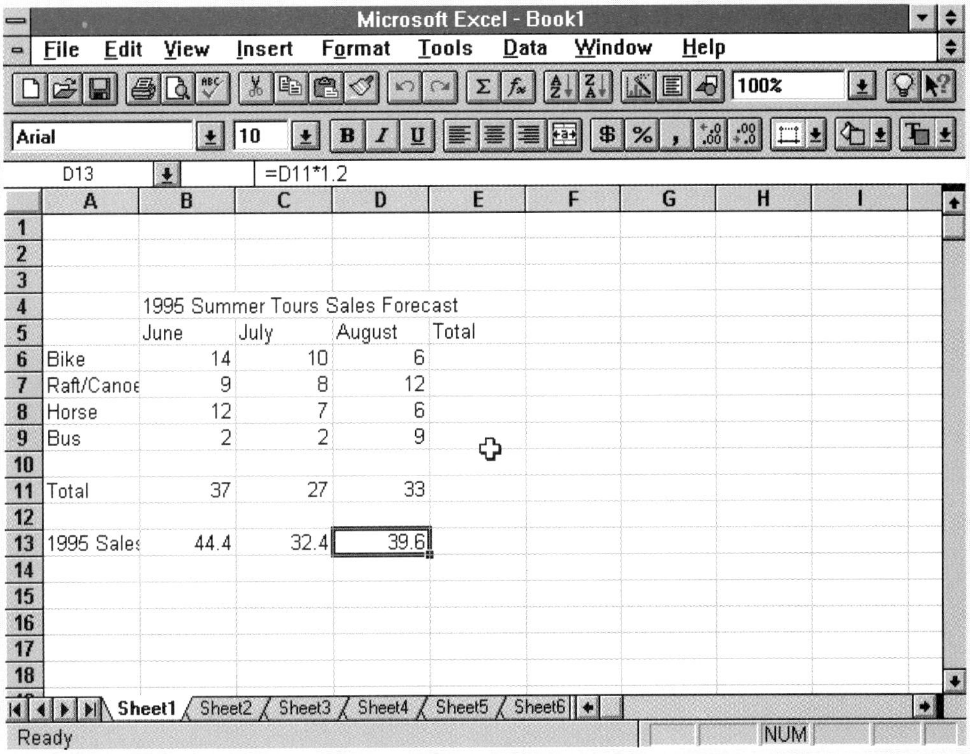

Order of precedence in Excel formulas

Each of the formulas for Evan's calculations involves only one arithmetic operator, but a formula can include several operations. When you work with formulas that have more than one operator, the **order of precedence** is very important. If a formula contains two or more operators, such as $4 + .55/4000 * 25$, the computer performs the calculations in a particular sequence based on these rules:

Calculated 1st   Calculation of exponents

Calculated 2nd   Multiplication and division, left to right

Calculated 3rd   Addition and subtraction, left to right

In the example $4 + .55/4000 * 25$, Excel performs the arithmetic operations in the following order. First, 4000 is divided into .55. Next Excel multiplies the result of .55/4000 by 25, then adds 4 to the result. You can change the order of calculations by using parentheses. Operations inside parentheses are calculated before any other operations.

Using Excel functions

Functions are predefined worksheet formulas that enable you to do complex calculations easily. Functions always begin with the formula prefix = (the equal sign). You can enter functions manually or you can use the Function Wizard. See the related topic "Using the Function Wizard" for more information. ▶ Evan uses the SUM function to calculate the grand totals in his worksheet.

1 Click cell **E6**
This is the cell where Evan wants to display the total of all bike tours for June, July, and August.

2 Position the pointer over the **AutoSum tool** Σ on the Standard toolbar
See the Figure 2-13. AutoSum sets up the SUM function to add the values in the cells above the cell pointer. If there are no values in the cells above the cell pointer, it adds the values in the cells to the left of the cell pointer—in this case, the values in cells B6, C6, and D6.

3 Click Σ
The formula =SUM(B6:D6) appears in the formula bar. The information inside the parentheses is the argument. An **argument** can be a value, a range of cells, text, or another function. After verifying that Excel has selected the correct range, Evan confirms the entry.

4 Click the **Enter button** ▨ on the formula bar
The result appears in cell E6. Next Evan calculates the total of raft and canoe tours.

5 Click cell **E7**, click Σ, then click ▨
Now he calculates the three-month total of the horse tours.

6 Click cell **E8** then click Σ
AutoSum sets up a function to sum the two values in the cells above the active cell. Evan needs to change the argument.

7 Click cell **B8** then drag to select the range **B8:D8**
As you drag, the argument in the SUM function changes to reflect the range being chosen.

8 Click ▨ to confirm the entry

9 Enter the SUM function in cells E9, E11 and E13
Make sure you add the values to the left of the active cell, not the values above it. See Figure 2-14.

TABLE 2-4: Frequently used functions

FUNCTION	DESCRIPTION
SUM(*argument*)	Calculates the sum of the arguments
AVERAGE(*argument*)	Calculates the average of the arguments
MAX(*argument*)	Displays the largest value among the arguments
MIN(*argument*)	Displays the smallest value among the arguments
COUNT(*argument*)	Calculates the number of values in the arguments

FIGURE 2-13:
AutoSum button

AutoSum ToolTip

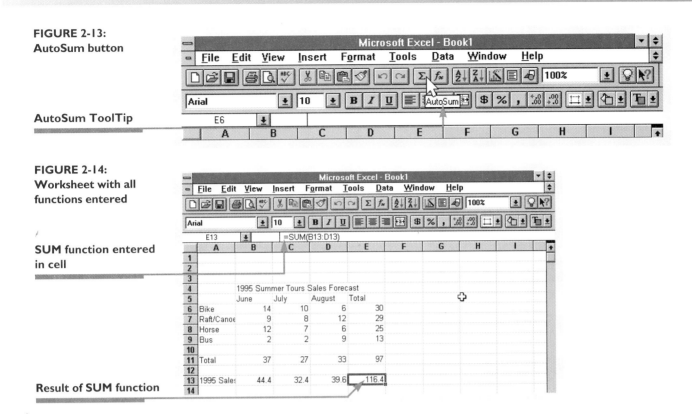

FIGURE 2-14:
Worksheet with all
functions entered

SUM function entered
in cell

Result of SUM function

Using the Function Wizard

The Function Wizard button [fx] is located to the right of the AutoSum button on the Standard toolbar. To use the Function Wizard, click [fx]. In the Function Wizard - Step 1 of 2 dialog box, shown in Figure 2-15, click the category containing the function you want, then click the desired function. The function appears in the formula bar. Click Next to display the Function Wizard - Step 2 of 2 dialog box, fill in values or cell addresses for the arguments, then click Finish.

Funtion Wizard button

Description of
selected functions

Click to fill in
arguments

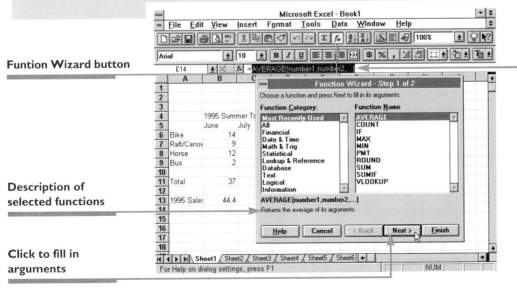

Functions and
arguments appear
in formula bar

FIGURE 2-15: First Function Wizard dialog box

QUICK **TIP**

If you are not sure
what a specific function
does, use the Function
Wizard to see a
description of its
function.■

Saving a workbook

As you might have learned in "Microsoft Windows 3.1" to store the workbook permanently, you must save it to a file on a disk. You should save your work every 10 to 15 minutes, especially before making significant changes in a workbook and before printing. For important files, you might want to save a copy of the file on a different disk. See the related topic "Creating backup files" for more information. You will save this file to the MY_FILES directory on your Student Disk. For more information about your Student Disk, refer to "Read This Before You Begin Microsoft Excel 5.0" on page 2 of this application. ▶ Evan wants to save his work.

1 Click **File** on the main menu bar, then choose **Save As**
   The Save As dialog box opens. See Figure 2-16. The text in the File Name text box is already selected.

2 Type **tours** to replace the default filename
   Filenames can contain up to eight characters. These characters can be lower- or uppercase letters, numbers, or any symbols except for spaces, commas, or the following symbols: . \ / [ ] " ^ : * ?.
   Excel automatically adds the .XLS extension to the filename.

3 Insert your Student Disk in the appropriate drive

4 Click the **Drives list arrow**, then click **a:**
   These lessons assume that your Student Disk is in drive A. If you are using a different drive or storing your practice files on a network, click the appropriate drive.

5 In the Directories list box, double-click the **MY_FILES** directory, then click **OK**
   If you don't have a MY_FILES directory, simply click OK. The Save As dialog box closes, and the Summary Info dialog box opens. As you create more files with Excel, you can use the Summary Info boxes to help you organize your files. For now, just click OK to close this dialog box.

6 Click **OK**
   The Summary Info dialog box closes, and the filename appears in the title bar at the top of the workbook. The workbook is saved to the MY_FILES directory on your Student Disk as a file named TOURS.XLS. Next, Evan enters his name at the top of the worksheet, so if others who use this worksheet have questions about it, they can ask him.

7 Click cell **A2**, type **Evan Brillstein**, then press **[Enter]**

8 Click **File** on the menu bar, then click **Save**
   This saves the changes made to a file that has already been named. Save a file frequently while working on it to protect all data. Table 2-5 shows the difference between the Save and the Save As commands.

FIGURE 2-16: Save As dialog box

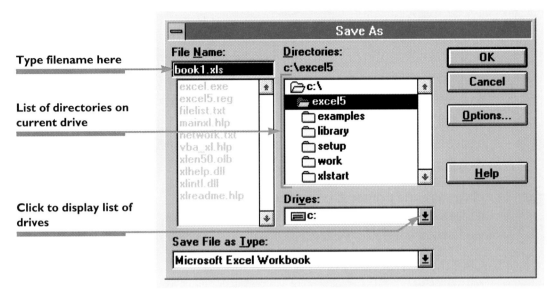

Type filename here

List of directories on
current drive

Click to display list of
drives

Creating backup files

It's good practice to back up your files in case something happens to your disk. To
create a backup copy of a file, save the file again to a second disk or with another
file extension such as .BAK.

TABLE 2-5:
The difference between the Save and Save As commands

COMMAND	DESCRIPTION	PURPOSE
Save As	Saves file, requires input name	To save a file the first time, to change the filename, or to save the file for use in a different application. Useful for backups.
Save	Saves named file	To save any changes to the original file. Fast and easy—do this often to protect your work.

Previewing and printing a worksheet

You print a worksheet when it is completed to have a paper copy to reference, file, or send to others. You can also print a worksheet that is not complete to review or work on when you are not at a computer. Before you print a worksheet, you should preview it. When you preview a worksheet, you see a copy of the worksheet exactly as it will appear on paper. You preview the worksheet to make sure that it will fit on a page before you print it. Table 2-6 provides printing tips. ▶ Evan previews and then prints a copy of the tours worksheet.

1   Make sure the printer is on and contains paper

If a file is sent to print and the printer is off, an error message appears. Evan previews the worksheet to check its overall appearance.

2   Click the **Print Preview tool** 🔍 on the Standard toolbar

You could also click File on the menu bar, then click Print Preview. A miniature version of the worksheet appears on the screen, as shown in Figure 2-17. If there were more than one page, you could click Next and Previous to move between pages. You can also enlarge the image by clicking the Zoom button. See the related topic "Using Zoom in Print Preview" for more information. After verifying that the preview image is correct, Evan prints the worksheet.

3   Click **Print**

The Print dialog box opens, as shown in Figure 2-18.

4   Make sure that the **Selected Sheet(s) radio button** is selected and that **1** appears in the Copies text box

Now Evan is ready to print the worksheet.

5   Click **OK**

The Printing dialog box appears while the file is sent to the printer. Note that the dialog box contains a Cancel button that you can use to cancel the print job.

6   Click **File** on the menu bar, then click **Close** to close the workbook

7   Click **File** on the menu bar, then click **Exit**

Excel closes and you are returned to the Program Manager window.

TABLE 2-6:
Worksheet printing guidelines

BEFORE YOU PRINT	RECOMMENDATION
Check the printer	Make sure the printer is on and on-line, that it has paper, and there are no error messages or warning signals.
Check the printer selection	Use the Printer Setup command in the Print dialog box to verify that the correct printer is selected.
Preview the worksheet	Check the formatted image for page breaks, page setup (vertical or horizontal), and overall appearance of the worksheet.

FIGURE 2-17:
Print Preview screen

Move to another page

Enlarge the screen
image

Print the worksheet

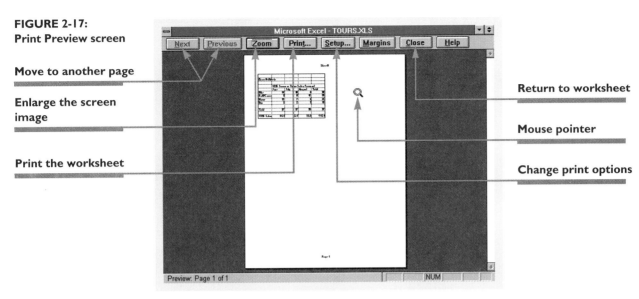

Return to worksheet

Mouse pointer

Change print options

FIGURE 2-18:
Print dialog box

Choose to print the
current worksheet

Set the number of
copies here

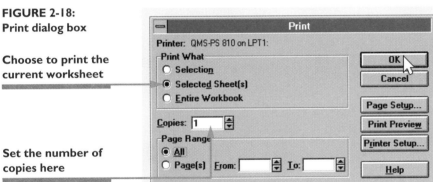

Using Zoom in Print Preview

When you are in the Print Preview window, you can make the image of the page
larger by clicking the Zoom button. You can also position the mouse pointer over
a specific part of the worksheet page, then click it to view that section of the page.
While the image is zoomed in, use the scroll bars to view different sections of the
page. See Figure 2-19.

Scroll bars

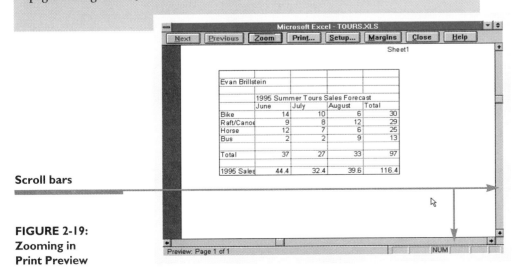

FIGURE 2-19:
Zooming in
Print Preview

QUICK **TIP**

You should save your
worksheet prior to
printing, so if anything
happens to the file as
it is being sent to the
printer, you will have
a clean copy saved to
your disk.■

CONCEPTSREVIEW

Label each of the elements of the Excel worksheet window shown in Figure 2-20.

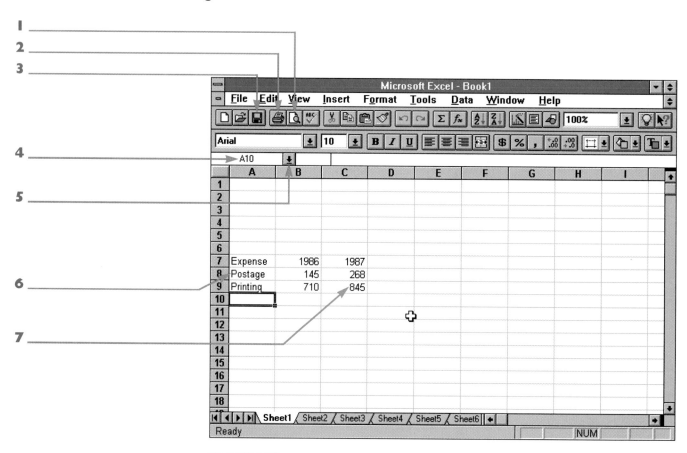

FIGURE 2-20

Match each of the terms with the statement that describes its function.

8 A predefined formula that provides a shortcut for commonly used calculations

9 A cell entry that performs a calculation in an Excel worksheet

10 A specified group of cells, which can include the entire worksheet

11 The location of a particular cell in a worksheet, identified by a column letter and row number

12 The character that identifies a value as a label

a. Range

b. Function

c. Cell address

d. Apostrophe

e. Formula

Select the best answer from the list of choices.

13 All of the following confirm an entry in a cell, EXCEPT:

a. Clicking the Cancel button

b. Clicking the Enter button

c. Pressing [Enter]

d. Pressing [↓]

14 The first character in any Excel formula is

a. *

b. /

c. =

d. @

APPLICATIONSREVIEW

1 Enter labels and save a workbook.

a. Start Excel and make sure you have an empty workbook in the Excel worksheet window.

b. Name Sheet1 tab Funds.

c. Save the workbook as FUNDS.XLS to the MY_FILES directory on your Student Disk.

d. Type "Total" in cell A6, then press [Enter].

e. Click cell B1 then type "SHARES."

f. Click the Enter button ■ on the formula bar to enter Shares in cell B1.

g. Press [→] to move to C1, then type "PRICE."

h. Press [Tab] to move to cell D1.

i. Type "Sold" then press [Esc]. Note that the entry disappears from the cell. Leave cell D1 blank.

j. Save your work.

2 Enter values and name ranges.

a. Enter the four mutual funds labels and values from Table 2-7 into the range A1:C5 in the Funds worksheet.

TABLE 2-7

	SHARES	PRICE
Arch	210	10.01
RST	50	18.45
United	100	34.50
Vista	65	11.15

b. Name range B2:B5 Shares.

c. Name range C2:C5 Price.

d. Save, then preview and print the worksheet.

3 Enter formulas, then preview and print the worksheet.

a. Click cell B6.

b. Enter the formula B2+B3+B4+B5.

c. Save your work, then preview and print the data in the Funds worksheet.

4 Use Excel functions.

a. Click cell C7.

b. Enter the function AVERAGE(C2..C5).

c. Type the label "Average Price" in cell A7.

d. Save your work.

e. Preview and print this worksheet.

f. Close the workbook.

5 Build a simple check register to balance a checkbook. Set up the worksheet using the data from Table 2-8 in a new workbook.

TABLE 2-8

CHECK NO.	DATE	DESC	AMOUNT
1601	June 17	Cleaning	12.65
1602	June 29	Tickets	38.02
1603	July 18	Cable	14.50
1604	July 25	Food	47.98

a. Click the New Workbook button ▢ to open a new workbook.

b. Name Sheet1 tab Checkbook.

c. Enter the label "Check Register" in cell A1.

d. Enter the column labels in the range A3:D3.

e. Enter all four check numbers, with the corresponding dates, descriptions, and amounts in the range A4:D7. Don't worry if the format of the date entries changes.

f. Generate a total of the check amounts you have entered. Enter the function SUM(D4..D7) in cell D8. Enter the label "Total" in cell A8.

g. Save the workbook as CHECK.XLS, then preview and print the worksheet.

6 Edit cell entries and preview the worksheet.

a. Change the description for check 1601 to Laundry.

b. Click cell D5, click in the formula bar, then edit the amount for check 1602 to 43.62.

c. Click cell D6, press [F2], then edit the amount for check 1603 to 23.22.

d. Save your work, preview and print the worksheet, then close the workbook.

7 Develop a worksheet that calculates the weekly payroll for Suncoast Security Systems. Open a new workbook and set up the worksheet using the data from Table 2-9.

TABLE 2-9

EMPLOYEE	HOURS WORKED	HOURLY WAGE	GROSS PAY
D. Hillman	32	9	
S. Lipski	25	12	
L. Skillings	40	7	

a. Click the New Workbook button ▢ to open a new workbook.

b. Enter the column labels, beginning in cell A2. Use two rows for the labels.

c. Enter the employee names, hours worked, and wage information using Table 2-9.

d. Enter the formula B4+B5+B6 in cell B7 to calculate the total hours worked.

e. Name Sheet1 tab Suncoast.

f. Save your workbook as SUNSEC.XLS to your MY_FILES directory, then preview and print the worksheet.

INDEPENDENT
CHALLENGE 1

You are the box office manager for Lightwell Players, a regional theater company. Your responsibilities include tracking seasonal ticket sales for the company's main stage productions and anticipating ticket sales for the next season. Lightwell Players sell four types of tickets: reserved seating, general admission, senior citizen tickets, and student tickets.

The 1993-94 season included productions of *Hamlet, The Cherry Orchard, Fires in the Mirror, The Shadow Box,* and *Heartbreak House.*

Open a new workbook and save it as THEATER.XLS to the MY_FILES directory on your Student Disk. Plan and build a worksheet that tracks the sales of each of the four ticket types for all five of the plays. Calculate the total ticket sales for each play, the total sales for each of the four ticket types, and the total sales for all ticket types.

Enter your own sales data, but assume the following: the Lightwell Players sold 800 tickets during the season; reserved seating was the most popular ticket type for all of the shows except for *The Shadow Box*; no play sold more than 10 student tickets. Plan and build a second worksheet in the workbook that reflects a 5% increase in all ticket types.

To complete this independent challenge:

1 Think about the results you want to see, the information you need to build these worksheets, and what types of calculations must be performed.

2 Sketch sample worksheets on a piece of paper indicating how the information should be laid out. What information should go in the columns? In the rows?

3 Build the worksheets by entering a title, row labels, column headings, and formulas. Use named ranges to make the worksheet easier to read, and rename the sheet tabs to easily identify the contents of each sheet. (*Hint:* If your columns are too narrow, position the cell pointer in the column you want to widen. To widen the column, click Format on the menu bar, click Column, click Width, choose a new column width, then click OK.)

4 Use separate worksheets for the ticket sales and projected sales showing the 5% increase.

5 Save your work, then preview and print the worksheets.

6 Submit your sketches and printed worksheets.

INDEPENDENT
CHALLENGE 2

You have been promoted to Computer Lab Manager at your school, and it is your responsibility to make sure there are enough computers for students during scheduled classes. Currently, you have four classrooms: three with IBM PC's and one with Macintoshes. Classes are scheduled Monday, Wednesday, and Friday in two-hour increments from 9AM to 5PM (the lab closes at 7PM) and each room can currently accommodate 20 computers.

Open a new workbook and save it as LABMNGR.XLS. Plan and build a worksheet that tracks the number of students who can currently use available computers per two-hour class. Create your enrollment data, but assume that current enrollment averages at 85% of each room's daily capacity. Using an additional worksheet, show the impact of an enrollment increase of 25%. To complete this independent challenge:

1 Think about how to construct these worksheets to create the desired output.

2 Sketch sample worksheets on a piece of paper, indicating how the information should be laid out.

3 Build the worksheets by entering a title, row labels, column headings, and formulas. Use named ranges to make the worksheet easier to read, and rename the sheets to easily identify their contents.

4 Use separate sheets for actual enrollment and projected changes.

5 Save your work, then preview and print the worksheets.

6 Submit your sketches and printed worksheets.

▶ Open an existing workbook

▶ Insert and delete rows and columns

▶ Copy and move cell entries

▶ Copy and move formulas

▶ Copy formulas with absolute references

▶ Adjust column widths

▶ Format values

▶ Format cell data with fonts and point sizes

▶ Format cell data with attributes and alignment

Modifying
A WORKSHEET

uilding on your ability to create a worksheet and enter data into it, you will now learn how to insert and delete columns and rows, move, copy, paste and format cell contents, and resize columns. ▶ The marketing managers at Nomad Ltd told Evan Brillstein that it would be helpful to have forecasts for the entire year, so Evan prepared a worksheet containing the forecast for the Spring and Fall Tours Sales and another worksheet with the forecast for the Winter Tours Sales. He created these new worksheets as Sheet2 and Sheet3 in the workbook containing the 1995 Summer Tours Sales Forecast. Having three related worksheets in one workbook makes it easier for Evan to compare them. ▶

Opening an existing workbook

Sometimes it's useful to create a new worksheet by modifying one that already exists. This saves you from having to retype information. Throughout this book, you will be instructed to open a file from your Student Disk, use the Save As command to create a copy of the file with a new name, and then modify the new file by following the lesson steps. Saving the files with new names keeps your original Student Disk files intact in case you have to start the lesson over again or you wish to repeat an exercise. ▶ Follow as Evan opens his 1995 Tours Forecast workbook, then uses the Save As command to create a copy with a new name.

1   Start Excel then click the **Open button** 🖻 on the Standard toolbar
The Open File dialog box opens. See Figure 3-1. Notice that it is very similar to the Save As dialog box you saw in Unit 2.

2   Click the **Drives list arrow**
A list of the available drives appears. Locate the drive that contains your Student Disk. In these lessons we assume your Student Disk is in drive A.

3   Click **a:**
A list of the files on your Student Disk appears in the File Name list box, with the default filename placeholder in the File Name text box already selected.

4   In the File Name list box, click **UNIT_3-1.XLS**, then click **OK**
The file UNIT_3-1.XLS opens. You could also double-click the filename in the File Name list to open the file. To create and save a copy of this file with a new name, Evan uses the Save As command.

5   Click **File** on the menu bar, then click **Save As**
The Save As dialog box opens.

6   Make sure the Drives list box displays the drive containing your Student Disk, then double-click MY_FILES in the list of directories
You should save all your files to your Student Disk in the MY_FILES directory, unless instructed otherwise. If you do not have a MY_FILES directory, simply save the file to your Student Disk.

7   In the File Name text box, select the current filename (if necessary), then type **TOURINFO**
See Figure 3-2.

8   Click **OK** to close the Save As dialog box and save the file, then click **OK** again to close the Summary Info dialog box if necessary
The file UNIT_3-1.XLS closes, and a duplicate file named TOURINFO.XLS is now open.

FIGURE 3-1: Open File dialog box

Selected filename

List of filenames will
appear here

Click to display list of
available drives

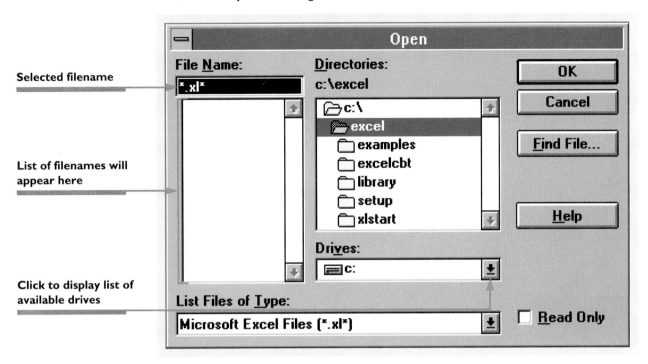

FIGURE 3-2: Save As dialog box

Type new filename
here

Current drive and
directory

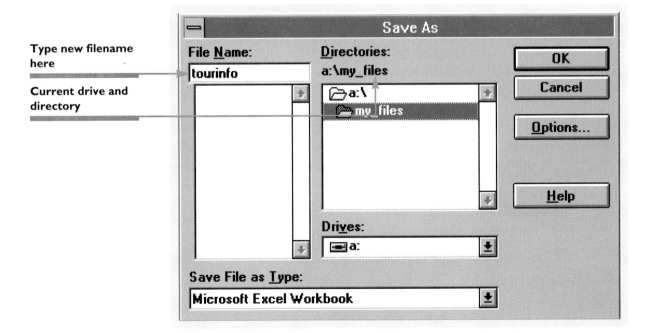

TROUBLE?

All lessons from this
point on assume you
have Excel running. If
you need help starting
Excel, refer to Unit 1.■

Inserting and deleting rows and columns

As you modify a worksheet, you might find it necessary to insert or delete rows and columns. For example, you might need to insert rows to accommodate new inventory products or remove a column of yearly totals that are no longer current. Inserting or deleting rows or columns can help to make your worksheet more attractive and readable. Inserting or deleting rows or columns can also cause problems with formulas that reference cells in that area. For information on how to avoid these problems, see the related topic "Using dummy columns and rows." ▶ Evan has already improved the appearance of his worksheet by using the Bold button to format the column headings. Now, he decides to insert a row between the worksheet title and the column labels. Evan also decides to discontinue bus tours for the 1995 summer season because of slow sales in 1994, so he needs to delete the row containing bus tour information.

1   Double-click the **Sheet1 tab**, then name it **Summer**
This will identify this sheet of the workbook.

2   Click cell **A5**, click **Insert** on the menu bar, then click **Cells**
The Insert dialog box opens. See Figure 3-3. You can choose to insert a column or a row, or you can shift the data in the cells in the active column right or in the active row down. Evan wants to insert a row to add some space between the title and column headings.

3   Click the **Entire Row radio button**, then click **OK**
A blank row is inserted between the title and the month labels. When you insert a new row, the contents of the worksheet shifts down from the newly inserted row. When you insert a new column, the contents of the worksheet shifts to the right from the point of the new column. Now Evan deletes the row containing information about bus sales. Because the formulas in row 12 use ranges whose **anchors** (cells used in the range address) are in row 10 (the bus sales row), he can't delete row 10 without having to change the formulas. To get around this problem, he clears the data from row 10, then he deletes the blank row 11 so the worksheet doesn't have two blank rows together.

4   Select the range **A10:E10**, containing the bus tour information

5   Click **Edit** on the menu bar, click **Clear**, then click **All**
The data in the range A10:E10 disappears. Notice that the formula results in rows 12 and 14 are adjusted because of the deletion of bus tour sales. Now delete a blank row.

6   Click the **row 11 selector button** (the gray box containing the row number to the left of the worksheet)
All of row 11 is selected as shown in Figure 3-4.

7   Click **Edit** in the menu bar, then click **Delete**
Excel deletes row 11, and all rows below this shift up one row. Evan is satisfied with the appearance of his worksheet and decides to save the changes.

8   Click the **Save button** 🖫 on the Standard toolbar

FIGURE 3-3:
Insert dialog box

Click to insert row

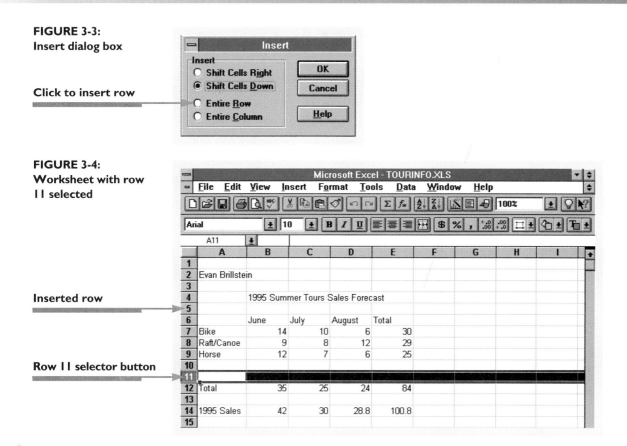

FIGURE 3-4:
Worksheet with row
11 selected

Inserted row

Row 11 selector button

Using dummy columns and rows

You use cell references and ranges in formulas. When you add or delete a column or row *within* a range used in a formula, Excel automatically adjusts the formula to reflect the change. However, when you add a column or row at the *end* of a range used in a formula, you must modify the formula to reflect the additional column or row. To eliminate having to edit the formula, you can include a dummy column and dummy row in the range you need to use in the formula. A **dummy column** or **dummy row** is a blank column or row included at the end of a range, as shown in Figure 3-5. Then if you add another column or row to the end of the range, the formula will automatically be modified to include the new data.

FIGURE 3-5: Formula
with dummy row

Formula with dummy
row

Dummy row

Rows included in
formula

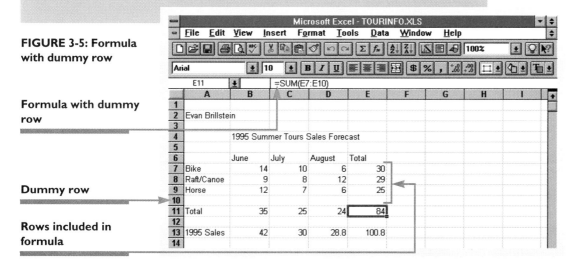

Copying and moving cell entries

Moving and Copying Text

Using the Cut, Copy, and Paste buttons or Excel's drag-and-drop feature, you can copy or move information from one cell or range in your worksheet to another. You can also cut, copy, and paste data from one worksheet to another. For information on adding and deleting worksheets, see the related topic on the next page. ▶ Evan included the 1995 forecast for Spring and Fall Tours Sales in his TOURINFO workbook. He already entered the spring report in Sheet2 and will finish entering the labels and data for the fall report. Using the Copy and Paste buttons and drag-and-drop, Evan copies information from the spring report to the fall report.

1 Double-click the **Sheet2 tab** then rename it **Spring-Fall**
Don't worry if you can't see all of the labels. You will fix this later. First, Evan copies the labels identifying the types of tours from the spring report to the fall report.

2 Select the range **A4:A9**, then click the **Copy button** 📑 on the Standard toolbar
The selected range (A4:A9) is copied to the Clipboard. The **Clipboard** is a temporary storage file that holds all the selected information you copy or cut. The Cut button ✂ would remove the selected information and place it on the Clipboard. To copy the contents of the Clipboard to a new location, you click a new cell, then use the Paste command.

3 Click cell **A13** then click the **Paste button** 📋 on the Standard toolbar
The contents of the Clipboard is copied into the range A13:A18. When pasting the contents of the Clipboard into the worksheet, you need to specify only the first cell of the range where you want the copied selection to go. Evan decides to use drag-and-drop to copy the Total label.

4 Click cell **E3** then position the pointer on any edge of the cell until the pointer changes to ⇖

5 While the pointer is ⇖ , press and hold down **[Ctrl]**
The pointer changes to ⇖⁺ .

6 While still pressing **[Ctrl]**, press and hold the **left mouse button** then drag the cell contents to cell **E12**
As you drag, an outline of the cell moves with the pointer, as shown in Figure 3-6. When you release the mouse button, the Total label appears in cell E12. Evan now decides to move the worksheet title over to the left. To use drag-and-drop to move, rather than copy, data to a new cell, do not press [Ctrl].

7 Click cell **C1**, then position the mouse on the edge of the cell until it changes to ⇖ , then drag the cell contents to **A1**
Evan enters fall sales data into the range B13:D16, as shown in Figure 3-7.

8 Using the information shown in Figure 3-7, enter the sales data for the fall tours into the range **B13:D16**
Compare your worksheet to Figure 3-7, then continue to the next lesson.

FIGURE 3-6: Using drag-and-drop to copy information

Cut button

Copy button

Paste button

Copied cell

Outline of copied cell

Drag-and-drop pointer to copy data

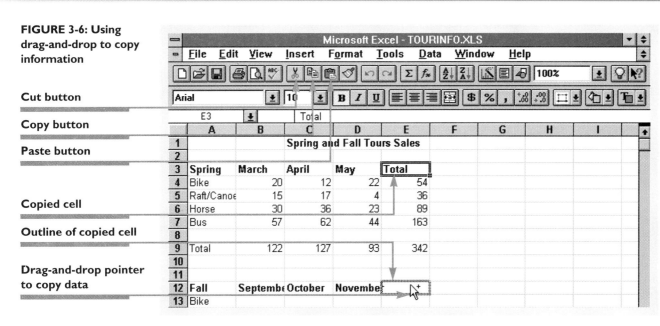

FIGURE 3-7: Worksheet with fall tours data entered

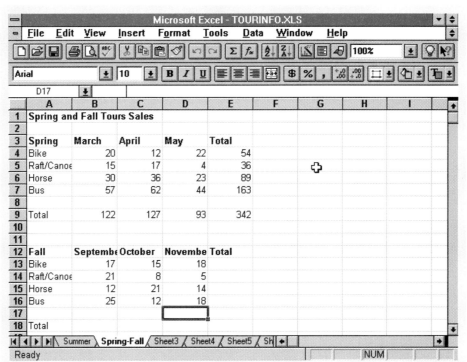

Adding and deleting worksheets

You can add or delete worksheets as necessary. To add a worksheet, click Insert on the menu bar, then click Worksheet. A new worksheet is added immediately *before* the active worksheet. To delete a worksheet, click Edit on the menu bar, then click Delete Sheet. The active worksheet is deleted, and the worksheet immediately *after* becomes the active worksheet.

TROUBLE?

When you drag-and-drop into occupied cells, you will be asked if you want to replace the existing cells. Click OK to replace the contents with the cell you are moving.■

Copying and moving formulas

Copying and moving formulas allows you to reuse formulas you've already created. Copying formulas, rather than retyping them, helps prevent new typing errors. ▶ Evan wants to copy the formulas that total the types of tours and that add the tours per month from the spring tours report to the fall tours report.

1 Click cell **E4** then click the **Copy button** 🖺 on the Standard toolbar
The formula for calculating the total number of spring bike tours is copied to the Clipboard. Notice that the formula in the formula bar appears as =SUM(B4:D4).

2 Click cell **E13** then click the **Paste button** 🖺 on the Standard toolbar
The formula from cell E4 is copied into cell E13. A new result of 50 appears in E13. Notice in the formula bar that the cell references have changed, so that the range B13:D13 appears in the formula. Formulas in Excel contain relative cell references. A **relative cell reference** tells Excel to copy the formula to a new cell, but to substitute new cell references that are in the same relative position to the new formula location. In this case, Excel inserted cells D13, C13 and B13, the three cell references immediately to the left of E13.

Notice that the bottom right corner of the active cell contains a small square, called the **fill handle**. Evan uses the fill handle to copy the formula in cell E13 to cells E14, E15, and E16. You can also use the fill handle to copy labels. See the related topic "Filling ranges with a series of labels" for more information.

3 Position the pointer over the fill handle until it changes to **+**

4 Drag the fill handle to select the range **E13: E16**
See Figure 3-8.

5 Release the mouse button
Once you release the mouse button, the fill handle copies the formula from the active cell (E13) and pastes it into each cell of the selected range. Again, because the formula uses relative cell references, cells E14 through E16 correctly display the totals for raft and canoe, horse, and bus tours.

FIGURE 3-8: Selected range using the fill handle

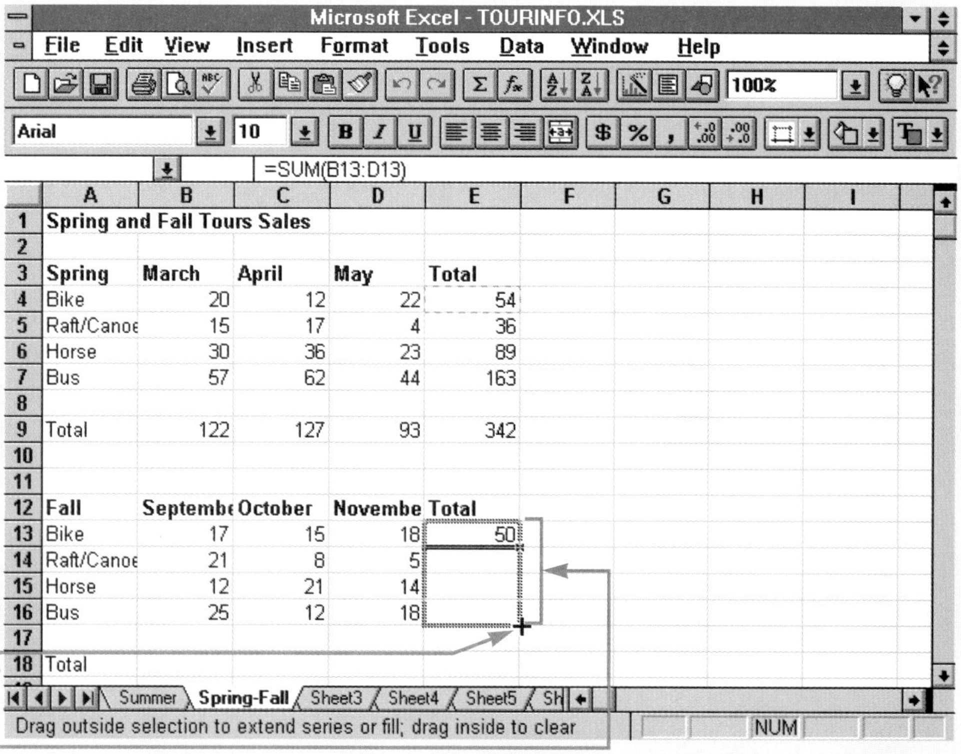

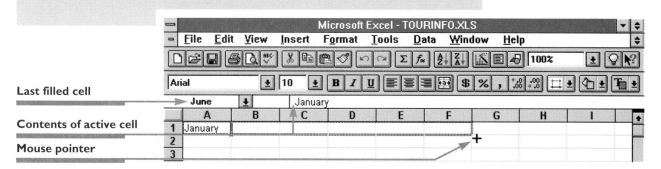

Mouse pointer

Formula in E13 will be
copied to E14:E16

Filling ranges with a series of labels

You can fill cells with a series of labels using the fill handle. You can fill cells with sequential months, days of the week, years, and text plus a number (Quarter 1, Quarter 2,...). Figure 3-9 shows a series of months being created with the fill handle. As you drag the fill handle, the contents of the last filled cell appears in the name box. You can also use the Fill Series command on the Edit menu.

Last filled cell

Contents of active cell

Mouse pointer

FIGURE 3-9: Using the fill handle to create a label series

QUICK **TIP**

Use the Fill Series command on the Edit menu to examine all of Excel's available fill series options.■

Copying and moving formulas, continued

To complete the fall tours section of his worksheet, Evan now must copy the formulas from the range B9:E9 to the range B18:E18. To do this, he'll use the Copy and Paste commands and the Fill Right command.

6 Click cell **B9**, click **Edit** on the menu bar, then click **Copy**
   The Copy command on the Edit menu has the same effect as clicking the Copy button 📋 on the Standard toolbar. See Table 3-1 for Cut, Copy, Paste, and Undo shortcuts.

7 Click cell **B18**, click **Edit** on the menu bar, then click **Paste**
   See Figure 3-10. The formula for calculating the September tours sales appears in the formula bar. You can also cut, copy, and paste among sheets in a workbook. Now Evan uses the Fill Right command to copy the formula from cell B18 to cells C18, D18, and E18.

8 Select the range **B18:E18**

9 Click **Edit** on the menu bar, click **Fill**, then click **Right**
   The rest of the totals are filled in correctly. Compare your worksheet to Figure 3-11.

10 Click the **Save button** 💾 on the Standard toolbar

TABLE 3-1: Cut, Copy, Paste, and Undo shortcuts

TOOL	KEYBOARD	MENU COMMAND	DESCRIPTION
✂️	[Ctrl][X]	Edit Cut	Deletes the selection from the cell or range and places it on the Clipboard
📋	[Ctrl][C]	Edit Copy	Copies the selection to the Clipboard
📋	[Ctrl][V]	Edit Paste	Pastes the contents of the Clipboard in the current cell or range
↩️	[Ctrl][Z]	Edit Undo	Undoes the last editing action

FIGURE 3-10:
Worksheet with
copied formula

Copied formula cell
references

Copied formula result

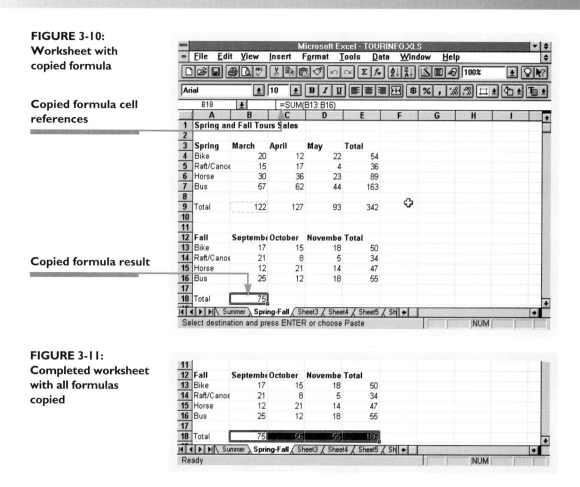

FIGURE 3-11:
Completed worksheet
with all formulas
copied

Using Find & Replace to edit a worksheet

If the worksheet is large and you need to make repeated changes to a work-sheet's labels or formulas, use the Replace command on the Edit menu to locate the data you want to change and change it. The Replace dialog box is shown in Figure 3-12. Enter the text, values, or formulas you want to change, called the **search criteria**, in the Find What text box. In the Replace with text box, enter the text, values, or formulas you want to replace the search criteria. Click Find Next to find the next occurrence of the search criteria, then click Replace to replace it with the replacement data, or click Replace All to replace all the instances of the search criteria in the workbook with the replacement data.

Type search criteria
here

Type replacement
data here

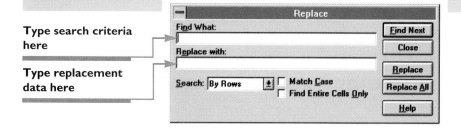

FIGURE 3-12: Replace dialog box

Copying formulas with absolute references

Relative versus Absolute Cell Referencing

Sometimes you might want a cell reference to always refer to a particular cell address. In such an instance, you would use an absolute cell reference. An **absolute cell reference** always refers to a specific cell address, even if you move the formula to a new location. You identify an absolute reference by placing a dollar sign ($) before the row letter and column number of the address (for example $A$1). ▶ Evan decides to add a column that calculates a possible increase in the number of spring tours in 1996. He wants to do a what-if analysis and recalculate the spreadsheet several times, changing the percentage that the tours might increase each time.

1   Click cell **G1**, type **Change**, then press **[→]**
Evan stores the increase factor that will be used in the what-if analysis in cell H1.

2   Type **1.1** in cell **H1**, then press **[Enter]**
This represents a 10% increase in sales.

3   Click cell **F3**, type **1996?**, then press **[Enter]**
Now, he creates a formula that uses an absolute reference to cell H1.

4   In cell F4, type **=E4*H1**, then click the **Enter button** ☒ on the formula bar
The result of 59.4 appears in cell F4. Evan now uses the fill handle to copy the formula in cell F4 to F5:F7.

5   Drag the fill handle to select the range **F4:F7**
The resulting values in the range F5:F7 are all zeros. When Evan looks at the formula in cell F5, which is =E5*H2, he realizes he needs to use an absolute reference to cell H1. Evan can correct this error by editing cell F4 using [F4], a shortcut key, to change the relative cell reference to an absolute cell reference.

6   Click cell **F4**, press **[F2]** to change to Edit mode, then press **[F4]**
Dollar signs appear, changing the H1 cell reference to absolute. See Figure 3-13.

7   Click the **Enter button** ☒ on the formula toolbar
Now that the formula correctly contains an absolute cell reference, Evan uses the fill handle to copy the formula in cell F4 to F5:F7.

8   Drag the fill handle to select the range **F4:F7**
Now Evan completes his what-if analysis by changing the value in cell H1 from 1.1 to 1.25 to indicate a 25% increase in sales.

9   Click cell **H1**, type **1.25**, then click the **Enter button** ☒ on the formula bar
The values in the range F4:F7 change. Compare your worksheet to Figure 3-14.

FIGURE 3-13: Absolute cell reference in cell F4

Absolute cell
reference in formula

Incorrect values due
to relative reference

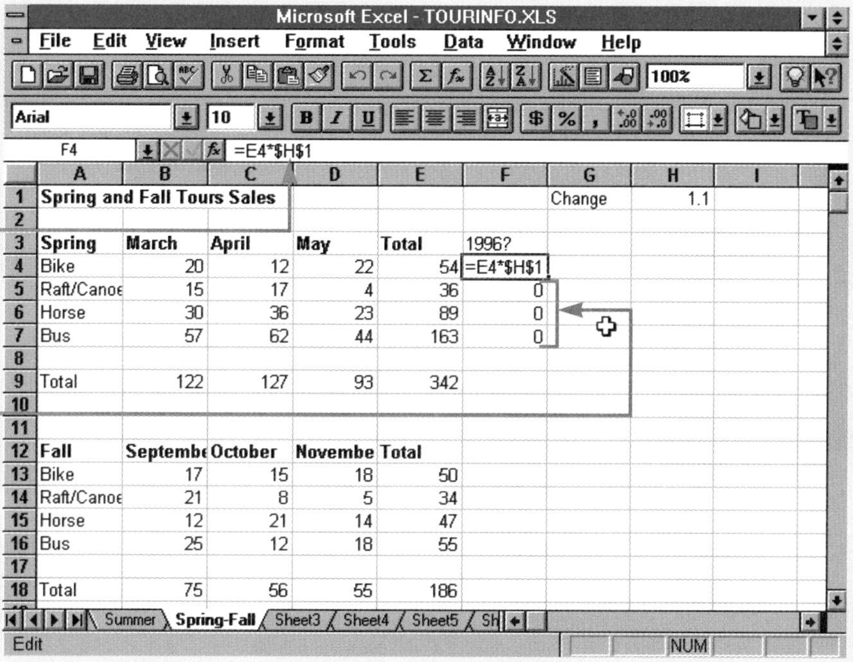

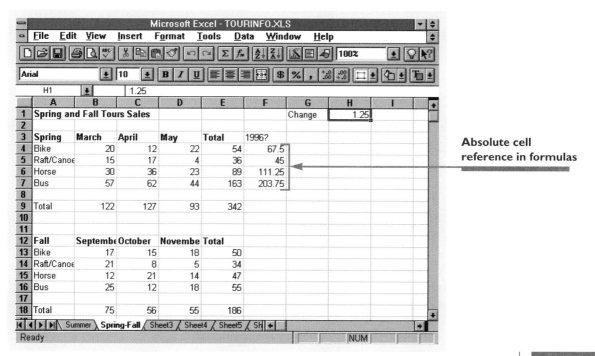

FIGURE 3-14: Worksheet with What-if value

Absolute cell
reference in formulas

QUICK **TIP**

Before you copy or
move a formula, check
to see if you need to
use an absolute cell
reference.■

Adjusting column widths

As you work with a worksheet, you might need to adjust the width of the columns to make your worksheet more usable. The default column width is 8.43 characters wide, a little less than one inch. With Excel, you can adjust the column width for one or more columns using the mouse or the Column command on the Format menu. Table 3-2 describes the commands available on the Format Column menu. You can also adjust the height of rows. See the related topic "Specifying row height" for more information. ▶ Evan notices that some of the labels in column A and the fall month names don't fit in the cells. He decides to adjust the widths of columns A, B, C, and D so that the labels fit in the cells.

1 Position the pointer on the column line between the columns A and B
   The pointer changes to ✛, as shown in Figure 3-15. Evan makes the column wider.

2 Drag the line to the right until column A is wide enough to accommodate all of the Raft/Canoe label
   Evan resizes the columns so they automatically accommodate the widest entry in a cell.

3 Position the pointer on the column line between columns B and C until it changes to ✛, then double-click the **left mouse button**
   The width of column B is automatically resized to fit the widest entry, in this case, September. This feature is called **AutoFit**. You use the Column Width command on the Format menu to adjust several columns to the same width.

4 Select the C, D, and E **column selector buttons** (the gray boxes containing the column letters just above the worksheet)

5 Click **Format** on the menu bar, click **Column**, then click **Width**
   The Column Width dialog box appears. See Figure 3-16. Move the dialog box, if necessary, by dragging it by its title bar so you can see the contents of the worksheet.

6 Type **10** in the Column Width text box, then click **OK**
   The column widths change to reflect the new settings. Evan is satisfied and decides to save his worksheet.

7 Click the **Save button** 🖫 on the Standard toolbar

TABLE 3-2:
Format Column commands

COMMAND	DESCRIPTION
Width	Sets the width to a specific number of characters
AutoFit Selection	Fits the widest entry
Hide	Hides column(s)
Unhide	Unhides column(s)
Standard Width	Resets to default widths

FIGURE 3-15: Preparing to change the column width

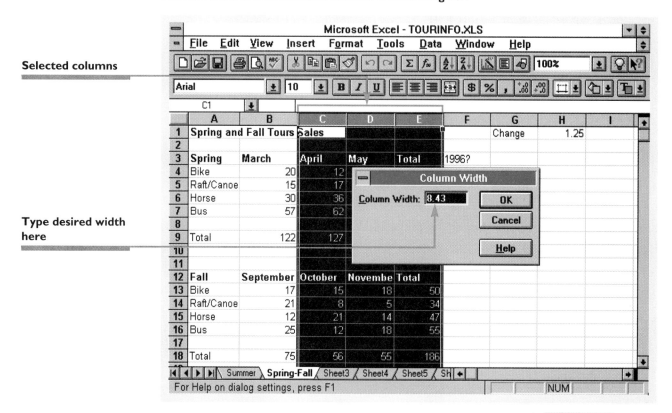

Mouse pointer between columns A and B

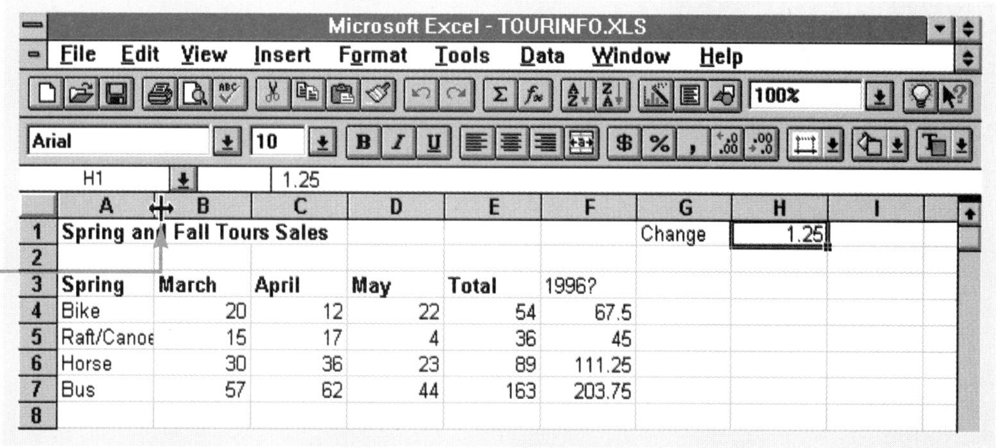

FIGURE 3-16: Worksheet with Column Width dialog box

Selected columns

Type desired width here

Specifying row height

The Row Height command on the Format menu allows you to customize row height to improve readability. Row height is calculated in **points**, units of measure also used for fonts—one inch equals 72 points. The row height must exceed the size of the font you are using. For example, if you are using a 12 point font, the row height must be more than 12 points. Normally, you don't need to adjust row heights manually. If you format something in a row to be a larger point size, Excel will adjust the row to fit the largest point size in the row.

QUICK **TIP**

To reset columns to the default width, select the range of cells, then use the Column Standard Width command on the Format menu. Click OK in the dialog box to accept the default width.■

Formatting values

Formatting is how information appears in cells; it does not alter the data in any way. To format a cell, you select it, then apply the formatting you want. You can also format a range of cells. Cells and ranges can be formatted before or after data is entered. If you enter a value in a cell, and the cell appears to display the data incorrectly, you need to format the cell to display the value correctly. You might also want more than one cell to have the same format. For more information on how to do this, see the related topic, "Using the Format Painter." ▶ The Marketing Department has also requested that Evan track tour advertising expenses. Evan developed a worksheet that tracks invoices for tour advertising. He formatted some of the values in the worksheet, and now he needs to finish.

1   Open the worksheet UNIT_3-2.XLS from your Student Disk, then save it as TOUR_ADS to your MY_FILES directory
Refer to the lesson "Opening an existing worksheet" in this unit if you need help. First, Evan wants to format the data in the Cost ea. column so it displays with a dollar sign.

2   Select the range **E4:E32**, then click the **Currency button** 💲 on the Formatting toolbar
Excel adds dollar signs and 2 decimal places to the Cost ea. column data. Columns G, H, and I contain dollar values also, but Evan doesn't want to repeat the dollar sign.

3   Select the range **G4:I32**, then click the **Comma button** 📓 on the Formatting toolbar
Column J contains percentages.

4   Select the range **J4:J32**, click the **Percentage button** 📊 on the Formatting toolbar, then click the **Increase Decimal tool** 📊 to show 1 decimal place
Data in the % of Total column is changed. Now Evan reformats the invoice dates.

5   Select the range **B4:B31**, click **Format** on the menu bar, then click **Cells**
The Format Cells dialog box appears with the Number tab in front. See Figure 3-17. You can also use this dialog box to format ranges with currency, comma, and percentages.

6   Select the format **d-mmm-yy** in the Format Codes list box, then click **OK**
The selected dates change in appearance, but they no longer fit in the cells. Evan also notices that the totals in row 32 of columns E and G are too wide for their cells. He needs to use AutoFit to widen these columns.

7   Position the pointer between columns B and C until it changes to ↔, then double-click the **left mouse button**; then double-click the **left mouse button** when ↔ is between columns E and F and between columns G and H
Evan doesn't need the year to appear in the Inv Due column.

8   Select the range **C4:C31**, click **Format** on the menu bar, click **Cells**, click **d-mmm** in the Format Codes list box, then click **OK**
Compare your worksheet to Figure 3-18. Now save the workbook.

9   Click the **Save button** 💾 on the Standard toolbar

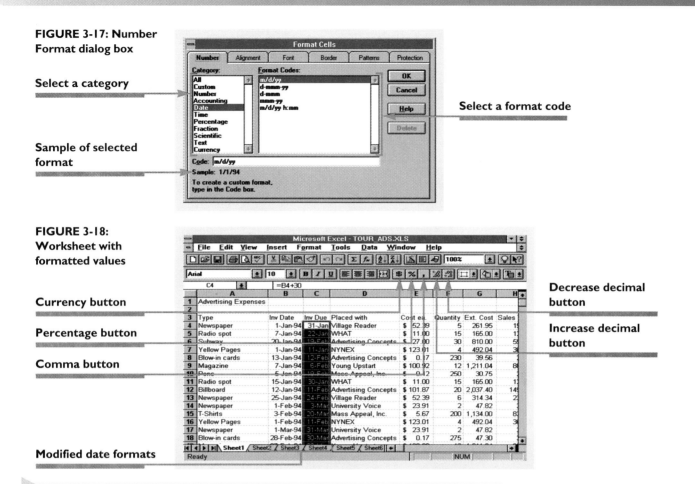

FIGURE 3-17: Number Format dialog box

Select a category

Sample of selected format

Select a format code

FIGURE 3-18:
Worksheet with formatted values

Currency button

Percentage button

Comma button

Modified date formats

Decrease decimal button

Increase decimal button

Using the Format Painter

A cell's format can be "painted" into other cells using the Format Painter button on the Formatting toolbar. This is similar to using drag-and-drop to copy information, but instead of copying cell contents, you copy only the cell format. Select the cell containing the desired format, then click. The pointer changes to, as shown in Figure 3-19. Use this pointer to select the cell or range you want to contain the painted format.

FIGURE 3-19: Using the Format Painter

	D	E	F	G	H	I	J	
19	Young Upstart	$ 100.92	12	1,211.04	88.65	1,299.69	7.4%	
20	Advertising Concepts	$ 27.00	30	810.00	59.29	869.29	5.0%	
21	WHAT	$ 11.00	30	330.00	24.16	354.16	2.0%	
22	Village Reader	$ 52.39	6	314.34	23.01	337.35	1.9%	
23	Advertising Concepts	$ 0.17	275	47.30	3.46	50.76	0.3%	
24	WHAT	$ 11.00	25	275.00	20.13	295.13	1.7%	
25	Mass Appeal, Inc.	$ 0.12	250	30.75	2.25	33.00	0.2%	
26	NYNEX	$ 123.01	4	492.04	36.02	528.06	3.0%	
27	Mass Appeal, Inc.	$ 7.20	250	1,800.00	131.76	1,931.76	11.0%	
28	Advertising Concepts	$ 27.00	30	810.00	59.29	869.29	5.0%	
29	University Voice	$ 23.91	2	47.82	3.50	51.32	0.3%	
30	Advertising Concepts	$ 27.00	30	810.00	59.29	869.29	5.0%	
31	Advertising Concepts	$ 101.87	20	2,037.40	149.14	2,186.54	12.5%	
32		$1,169.14	2034	16,311.75	1,194.02	17,505.77	100.0%	
33								
34								
35								
36								

Mouse pointer

Cell to be painted

Destination of painted format

TROUBLE?

If you don't see UNIT_3-2.XLS in the File Name list box in the Open dialog box, double-click the letter of the drive containing your Student Disk (probably drive A) in the Directories list box.■

Formatting cell data with fonts and point sizes

A **font** is the name given to a collection of characters (letters, numerals, symbols, and punctuation marks) with a specific design. The **point size** is the physical size of the text, measured in points. The default font in Excel is 10 point Arial. You can change the font, the size, or both of any entry or section in a worksheet by using the Format command on the menu bar or by using the Formatting toolbar. See the related topic, "Using the Formatting toolbar to change fonts and sizes" for more information on that method. Table 3-3 shows several fonts in different sizes.
▶ Evan wants to change the font and size of these labels to make the title and labels stand out.

1 Press **[Ctrl][Home]** to move to cell A1

2 Click **Format** on the menu bar, click **Cells,** then click the **Font tab**
See Figure 3-20. Evan decides to change the font of the title from Arial to Times New Roman, and he will increase the font size to 24.

3 Click **Times New Roman** in the Font list box, then click **24** in the Size list box, then click **OK**
If you don't have Times New Roman in your list of fonts, choose another font. The title font appears in 24 point Times New Roman, and the Formatting toolbar displays the new font and size information. Next, Evan makes the labels larger.

4 Select the range **A3:J3,** then click **Format** on the menu bar, then click **Cells**
The Font tab should still be the front-most tab.

5 Click **Times New Roman** in the Font list box, click **14** in the Size list box, then click **OK**

6 Resize the column widths in columns A through J so the larger labels fit in their cells
Compare your worksheet to Figure 3-21.

7 Click the **Save button** 🖫 on the Standard toolbar to save your formatting changes

TABLE 3-3: Types of fonts

FONT	12 POINT	24 POINT
Arial	Excel	Excel
Helvetica	Excel	Excel
Palatino	Excel	Excel
Times	Excel	Excel

FIGURE 3-20: Font tab of the Format Cells dialog box

Currently selected font

Available fonts on your computer

Sample of selected font

Effects options

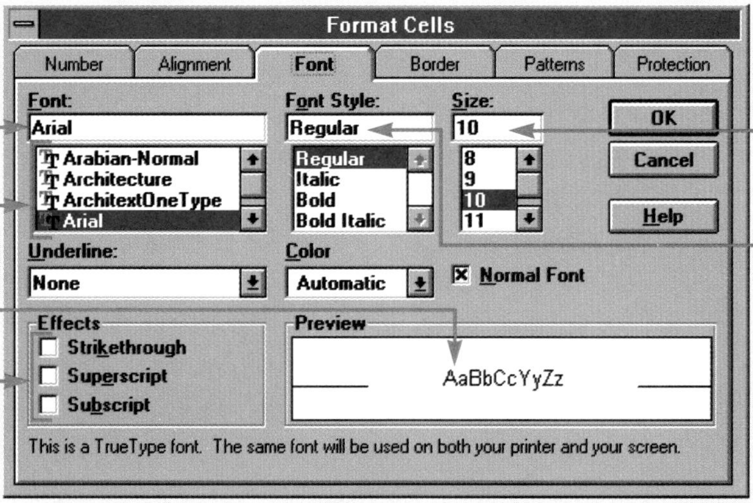

Type a custom size or select a size from the list

Formatting attribute options

FIGURE 3-21: Worksheet with enlarged title and labels

Title after changing to 24 point Times New Roman

Column headings now 14 point Times New Roman

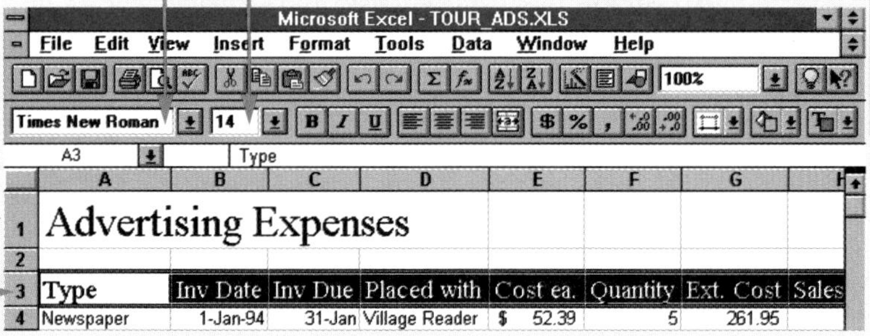

Font and size of active cell

Using the Formatting toolbar to change fonts and sizes

The font and size of the active cell appear on the Formatting toolbar. Click the Font list arrow, as shown in Figure 3-22, to see a list of available fonts. If you want to change the font, first select the text, click the Font list arrow, then choose the font you want. You can change the size of selected text in the same way, but click the Size list arrow to display a list of available point sizes.

Font list arrow

Size list arrow

Available fonts installed on your computer

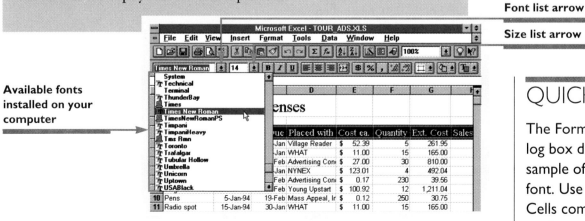

FIGURE 3-22: Available fonts on the Formatting toolbar

QUICK TIP

The Format cells dialog box displays a sample of the selected font. Use the Format Cells command if you're unsure of a font's appearance.■

Formatting cell data with attributes and alignment

Attributes are styling features such as bold, italics, and underlining. You can apply bold, italics, and underlining from the Formatting toolbar or from the Font tab of the Format Cells dialog box. You can also change the alignment of text in cells. Left, right, or center alignment can be applied from the Formatting toolbar, or from the Alignment tab of the Format Cells dialog box. See Table 3-4 for a description of the available attribute and alignment buttons. Excel also has predefined worksheet formats to make formatting easier; See the related topic "Using AutoFormat" for more information. ▶ Evan wants to further refine his worksheet by adding bold and underline formatting and centering some of the labels.

1   Click cell **A1** to select the title Advertising Expenses, then click the **Bold button** ⬛ on the Formatting toolbar

The title Advertising Expenses appears in bold.

2   Select the range **A3:J3**, then click the **Underline button** ⬛ on the Formatting toolbar

Excel underlines the labels in the selected range.

3   Click cell **A3**, click the **Italics button** ⬛ on the Formatting toolbar, then click ⬛

The word "Type" appears in boldface italic type. Notice that the Bold, Italics, and Underline buttons are depressed. Evan decides he doesn't like the italic formatting. He removes it by clicking ⬛ again.

4   Click ⬛

Excel removes italics from cell A3.

5   Add bold formatting to the rest of the labels in the range **B3:J3**

Evan wants to center the title over the data.

6   Select the range **A1:F1**, then click the **Center Across Columns button** ⬛ on the Formatting toolbar

The title Advertising Expenses is centered across 6 columns. Now Evan centers the column headings in their cells.

7   Select the range **A3:J3**, then click the **Center button** ⬛ on the Formatting toolbar

Evan is satisfied with the formatting on this worksheet so he saves his changes.

8   Click the **Save button** ⬛ on the Standard toolbar

Compare your screen to Figure 3-23. Highlighting information on a worksheet can be useful, but overuse of any attribute can be distracting and make a document less readable. Be consistent, adding emphasis the same way throughout a workbook.

9   Close the workbook then exit Excel

FIGURE 3-23: Worksheet with formatting attributes applied

Center button

Tools depressed

Column headings centered, bold, and underlined

Title centered across columns

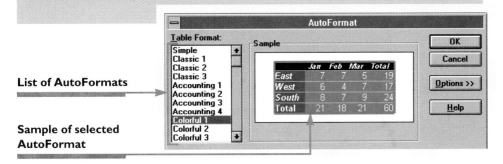

Using AutoFormat

Excel provides 16 preset formats called **AutoFormats**, which allow instant formatting of large amounts of data. AutoFormats are designed for worksheets with labels in the left column and top rows and totals in the bottom row or right column. To use AutoFormatting, select the data to be formatted, click Format on the menu bar, click AutoFormat, then select a format from the Table Format list box, as shown in Figure 3-24.

List of AutoFormats

Sample of selected AutoFormat

FIGURE 3-24: AutoFormat dialog box

TABLE 3-4: Formatting buttons

ICON	DESCRIPTION	ICON	DESCRIPTION
B	Adds boldface	≣	Aligns left
I	Italicizes	≣	Aligns center
U	Underlines	≣	Aligns right
▦	Adds lines or borders	▦	Centers across columns

QUICK **TIP**

When selecting a large, unnamed range, select the upper left-most cell in the range, press and hold [Shift], then click the lower right-most cell in the range.∎

CONCEPTSREVIEW

Label each of the elements of the Excel worksheet window shown in Figure 3-25.

1 _____

2 _____

3 _____

4 _____

5 _____

6 _____

7 _____

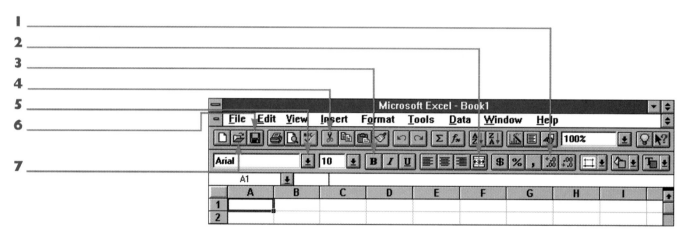

FIGURE 3-25

Match each of the statements to the command or button it describes.

8 Adds a new row or column

9 Erases the contents of a cell

10 Duplicates the contents of a cell

11 Changes the point size of selected cells

12 Pastes the contents of the Clipboard in the current cell

13 Changes the format to Currency

a. Format Cells

b. Edit Delete

c. Insert Row/Column

d. [clipboard icon]

e. [$ icon]

f. [paste icon]

Select the best answer from the list of choices.

14 When you copy data using the Copy button, Excel puts the selected data on the

a. Border

b. Menu

c. Clipboard

d. Range

15 A cell address that changes when copied into a new location is called a(n)

a. Absolute reference

b. Relative reference

c. Mixed reference

d. Combined reference

16 Cell D4 contains the formula =A4+B4+C4. If you copy this formula to cell D5, what will the formula be in cell D5?

a. =$A$4+$B$4+$C$4

b. =A4+B4+C4-D4

c. =D5-D4

d. =A5+B5+C5

APPLICATIONSREVIEW

1 Adjust column widths.

a. Open a new workbook.

b. Enter the information from Table 3-5 in your worksheet.

c. Adjust all columns widths using the AutoFit feature.

d. Save this workbook as CHAIRS.XLS to the MY_FILES directory on your Student Disk.

TABLE 3-5

Country Oak Chairs, Inc.

Quarterly Sales Sheet

Description	Price	Sold	TOTALS
Rocker	1299	1104	
Recliner	800	1805	
Bar stool	159	1098	
Dinette	369	1254	

2 Format cell data with new fonts and point sizes.

  a. Select the range of cells containing the column titles.

  b. Change the font of the column titles to Times New Roman.

  c. Increase the point size of the column titles to 14 point.

  d. Resize columns as necessary.

  e. Select the range of values in the Price column.

  f. Click the Currency button.

  g. Save your workbook changes.

3 Copy and move formulas.

  a. Enter the formula B4*C4 in cell D4. Adjust the number formatting, as needed.

  b. Copy the formula in cell D4 to cells D5, D6, D7, and D8.

  c. Adjust column widths as necessary.

  d. Save your workbook changes.

4 Format cell data with attributes and alignment.

  a. Select the worksheet title Country Oak Chairs, Inc.

  b. Click the Bold button to apply boldface to the title.

  c. Select the label Quarterly Sales Sheet.

  d. Click the Underline button to apply underlining to the label.

  e. Select the range of cells containing the column titles.

  f. Click the Align Center button to center the column titles.

  g. Resize the column widths as necessary to fit the data.

  h. Save your changes, then preview, and print the workbook.

5 Insert a row.

  a. Insert a new row between rows 4 and 5.

  b. Add Country Oak Chairs' newest product—a Shaker bench in the newly inserted row. Enter 239 for the price and 360 for the number sold.

  c. Use the fill handle to copy the formula in cell D4 to D5.

  d. Save your changes, then preview and print the workbook.

6 Format values.

  a. Open a new workbook.

  b. Enter the information from Table 3-6 in your worksheet. Type "National Public Radio" contributions in cell A1, then type the values in the range A2:C7.

  c. Use the Currency format to format the numbers in the Pledged column.

  d. Use the Percent format with no decimal places for the numbers in the % Received column.

  e. Change the width of the City column to 14 characters.

  f. Make the worksheet title bold.

  g. Save your workbook as NPR.XLS to the MY_FILES directory on your Student Disk, then preview and print it.

TABLE 3-6

National Public Radio contributions

City	Pledged	% Received
Honolulu	63000	.75
New York	42000	.63
San Francisco	45750	.54
Boston	52950	.52
Seattle	60000	.81

7 Open an existing workbook.

  a. Open the file UNIT_3-3.XLS from your Student Disk.

  b. Save it as RECAP.XLS to the MY_FILES directory on your Student Disk.

  c. Use the Bold button and Center button to format the column heads and row titles.

  d. Increase the point size of the column headings in row 3 to 12 point.

  e. Save your changes.

8 Copy formulas with absolute references.

  a. Type "5.7%" in cell H3, then format this cell as a percentage with one decimal place.

  b. Enter the formula F4*$H$3 in cell G4.

  c. Copy the formula in cell G4 to G5:G9 using any method.

  d. Save your changes, then preview and print the workbook.

  e. Close the workbook then exit Excel.

INDEPENDENT CHALLENGE 1

Write Brothers is a Houston-based company that manufactures high-quality pens and markers. As the finance manager, one of your responsibilities is to analyze the monthly reports from your five district sales offices. Your boss, Joanne Parker, has just told you to prepare a quarterly sales report for an upcoming meeting. Since several top executives will be attending this meeting, Joanne reminds you that the report must look professional. In particular, she asks you to emphasize the company's surge in profits during the last month and to highlight the fact that the Northeastern district continues to outpace the other districts.

Plan and build a worksheet that shows the company's sales during the last three months. Make sure you include:

- The number of pens sold (units sold) and the associated revenues (total sales) for each of the five district sales offices. The five Write Brothers sales districts include: Northeastern, Midwestern, Southeastern, Southern, and Western.
- Calculations that show month-by-month totals and a three-month cumulative total.
- Calculations that show each district's share of sales (percent of units sold).
- Formatting enhancements to emphasize the recent month's sales surge and the Northeast district's sales leadership.

To complete this independent challenge:

1 Prepare a worksheet plan that states your goal, lists the worksheet data you'll need, and identifies the formulas for the different calculations.

2 Sketch a sample worksheet on a piece of paper, indicating how the information should be organized and formatted. How will you calculate the totals? What formulas can you copy to save time and keystrokes? Do any of these formulas need to use an absolute reference? How will you show dollar amounts? What information should be shown in bold? Do you need to use more than one font? More than one point size?

3 Build the worksheet with your own sales data. Enter the titles and labels first, then enter the numbers and formulas. Save the workbook as WRITE.XLS to the MY_FILES directory on your Student Disk.

4 Make enhancements to the worksheet. Adjust the column widths as necessary. Format labels and values, and change attributes and alignment.

5 Add a column that calculates a 10% increase in sales. Use an absolute cell reference in this calculation.

6 Before printing, preview the file so you know what the worksheet will look like. Adjust any items as needed, and print a copy. Save your work before closing the file.

7 Submit your worksheet plan, preliminary sketches, and the final printout.

INDEPENDENT CHALLENGE 2

As the new computer lab manager of your class, you are responsible for all the computer equipment used in your classroom. In addition to knowing the current hardware and software capabilities and approximate capital costs, you must also be concerned with the number of hours the equipment is used, whether you would like to make any upgrades prior to the next semester, and those approximate costs. Plan and build a workbook that details the hardware and software used in your classroom. Make sure you include:

- The number of units and number of hours used
- Calculations that show the approximate value of hardware by unit and within the room
- The installed software and its total calculated value
- A "wish list" of hardware and software upgrades and their respective costs
- Formatting enhancements that emphasize the items or highest priority

To complete this independent challenge:

1 Prepare a worksheet plan that states your goal, lists the worksheet data you'll need, and identifies the formulas for the different calculations.

2 Sketch a sample worksheet on a piece of paper, indicating how the information should be formatted. What calculations are required? Can any of the formulas be copied? Do any of the formulas require an absolute reference? How will you make the numbers easy to read? What information should be shown in bold? Do you need to use more than one font? More than one point size?

3 Build the worksheet with the data you have gathered. Estimate the costs of hardware and software if you are unsure. Enter the titles and labels first, then enter the numbers and formulas. Save the workbook as LABCOSTS.XLS to the MY_FILES directory on your Student Disk.

4 Make enhancements to the worksheet. Format labels and values, and change attributes and alignment.

5 Before printing, preview the file so you know what the worksheet will look like. Adjust any items as needed, and print a copy. Save your work before closing the file.

6 Submit your worksheet plan, preliminary sketches, and the final printout.

UNIT 4

Working
WITH CHARTS

Worksheets provide an effective way to organize information, but they are not always the best format for presenting data to others. Information in a selected range or worksheet can be easily converted to the visual format of a chart. Charts quickly communicate the relationships of data in a worksheet. In this unit, you will learn how to create a chart, edit a chart and change the chart type, add text annotations and arrows to a chart, then preview and print it. ▶ Evan Brillstein needs to create a chart showing the six-month sales history at Nomad Ltd for the Annual Meeting. He wants to illustrate the impact of an advertising campaign that started in June. ▶

Planning and designing a chart

Choosing a Chart Type

Before creating a chart, you need to plan what you want your chart to show and how you want it to look. ▶ Evan wants to create a chart to be used at the Annual Meeting. The chart will show the spring and summer sales throughout the Nomad Ltd regions. In early June, the Marketing Department launched a national advertising campaign. The results of the campaign were increased sales for the summer months. Evan wants his chart to illustrate this dramatic sales increase.

Evan uses the worksheet shown in Figure 4-1 and the following guidelines to plan the chart:

1 **Determine the purpose of the chart, and identify the data relationships you want to communicate visually**
Evan wants to create a chart that shows sales throughout Nomad's regions in the spring and summer months (March through August). He particularly wants to highlight the increase in sales that occurred in the summer months as a result of the advertising campaign.

2 **Determine the results you want to see and decide which chart type is most appropriate to use; Table 4-1 describes several different types of charts**
Because he wants to compare related data (sales in each of the regions) over a time period (the months March through August), Evan decides to use a column chart.

3 **Identify the worksheet data you want the chart to illustrate**
Evan is using data from his worksheet titled "Nomad Ltd Regions, Spring and Summer Sales," as shown in Figure 4-1. This worksheet contains the sales data for the five regions from March through August.

4 **Sketch the chart then use this sketch to decide where the chart elements should be placed**
Evan sketches his chart as shown in Figure 4-2. He puts the months on the horizontal axis (the **x-axis**) and the monthly sales figures on the vertical axis (the **y-axis**). The **tick marks** on the y-axis create a scale of measure for each value. Each value in a cell he selects for his chart is a **data point**. In any chart, each data point is visually represented by a **data marker**, which in this case is a column. A collection of related data points is a **data series**. In Evan's chart, there are five data series (Midwest, Northeast, Northwest, South, and Southwest) so he has included a **legend** to identify them.

FIGURE 4-1:
Worksheet containing
sales data

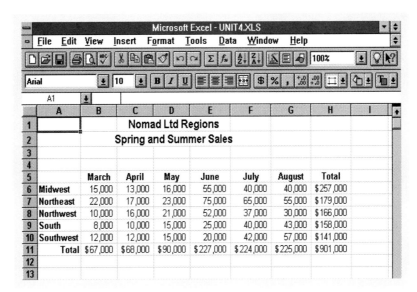

FIGURE 4-2:
Evan's sketch of
the column chart

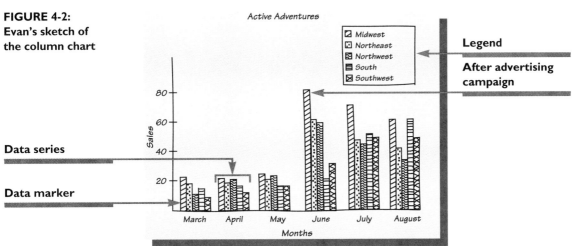

TABLE 4-1: Commonly used chart types

TYPE	BUTTON	DESCRIPTION
Area		Shows how volume changes over time
Bar		Compares distinct, unrelated objects over time using a horizontal format; sometimes referred to as a horizontal bar chart in other spreadsheet programs
Column		Compares distinct, unrelated objects over time using a vertical format; the Excel default; sometimes referred to as a bar chart in other spreadsheet programs
Line		Compares trends over even time intervals; similar to an area chart
Pie		Compares sizes of pieces as part of a whole; can have slices pulled away from the pie, or "exploded"
XY (scatter)		Compares trends over uneven time or measurement intervals; used in scientific and engineering disciplines for trend spotting and extrapolation
Combination	no button	Combines a column and line chart to compare data requiring different scales of measure

Creating a chart

To create a chart in Excel, you first select the range containing the data you want to chart. Once you've selected a range, you can use Excel's ChartWizard to lead you through the chart creation process. ▶ Using the worksheet containing the spring and summer sales data for the five regions, Evan will create a chart that shows the monthly sales of each region from March through August.

1 **Open the workbook UNIT_4-1.XLS from your Student Disk, then save it as REGIONS.XLS to the MY_FILES directory**
First, Evan needs to select the cells he wants to chart. He wants to include the monthly sales figures for each of the regions, but not the totals. He also wants to include the month and region labels.

2 **Select the range A5:G10, then click the ChartWizard button** 🖾 **on the Standard toolbar**
When you click the ChartWizard button, the pointer changes to ⁺ⱖ. See Figure 4-3. This pointer draws the border of the chart. Evan decides to place the chart directly below the worksheet.

3 **Position ⁺ⱖ so that the cross is at the top of cell A13, as shown in Figure 4-3, then drag the pointer to the lower-right corner of cell H24 to select the range A13:H24**
The first of five ChartWizard dialog boxes opens. This box confirms the range of data to be charted.

4 **Make sure the range is the same as the one you selected in Step 2, then click Next**
The second ChartWizard dialog box lets you choose the type of chart you want to create.

5 **Click Next to accept the default chart type of column**
The third dialog box lets you choose the format of the chart. Evan wants each region to have a different color bar, so he again accepts the default choice.

6 **Click Next**
The fourth ChartWizard dialog box shows a sample chart using the data you selected. Notice that the regions (the *rows* in the selected range) are plotted according to the months (the *columns* in the selected range), and that the months were added as labels for each data series. You could switch this by clicking the Columns radio button below Data Series on the right side of the dialog box. Notice also that there is a legend showing each region and its corresponding color on the chart.

7 **Click Next**
In the last ChartWizard dialog box, you can choose to keep the legend, add a chart title, and add axis titles. Evan adds a title.

8 **Click in the Chart Title text box, then type Nomad Ltd Regional Sales**
After a moment, the title appears in the Sample Chart box. See Figure 4-4.

9 **Click Finish**
The column chart appears in the defined plot area, as shown in Figure 4-5. Your chart might look slightly different. Just as Evan had hoped, the chart shows the dramatic increase in sales between May and June. The **selection handles**, the small black squares at the corners and sides of the chart's border, indicate that the chart is selected. Anytime a chart is selected (as it is now), the Chart toolbar appears. It might be floating, as shown in Figure 4-5, or it might be fixed at the top of the worksheet window.

FIGURE 4-3:
Worksheet with selected range and ChartWizard pointer

ChartWizard button depressed

ChartWizard pointer

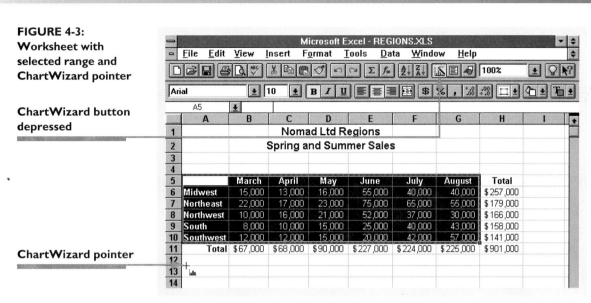

FIGURE 4-4:
Completed ChartWizard dialog box

Title added

Radio buttons for displaying legend

Miniaturized chart

Legend

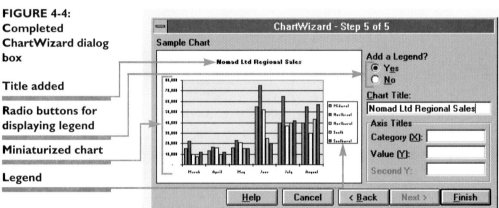

FIGURE 4-5:
Worksheet with column chart

Selection handles

Floating Chart toolbar

Title

Legend

Month labels on x-axis

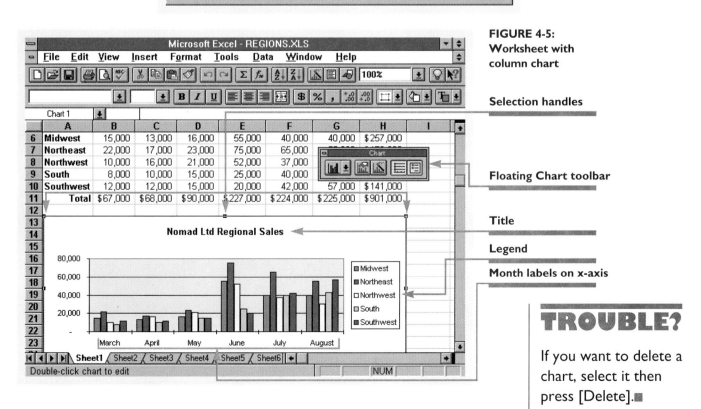

TROUBLE?

If you want to delete a chart, select it then press [Delete].■

Editing a chart

Once you've created a chart, it's easy to modify it. You can change data values in the worksheet, and the chart will automatically be updated to reflect the new data. You can also easily change chart types using the buttons on the Chart toolbar. Table 4-2 shows and describes the Chart toolbar buttons. ▶ Evan looks over his worksheet and realizes he entered the wrong data for the Northwest region in July and August. After he corrects this data, he wants to find out what percentage of total sales the month of June represents. He will convert the column chart to a pie chart to find this out.

1   Scroll the worksheet so that you can see both the chart and row 8, containing the Northwest region's sales figures, at the same time
    As you enter the correct values, watch the columns for July and August in the chart change to reflect the new data values.

2   Click cell **F8**, type **49000** to correct the July sales figure, press **[→]**, type **45000** in cell **G8**, then press **[Enter]**
    The Northwest columns for July and August reflect the increased sales figures. See Figure 4-6.

3   Select the chart by clicking anywhere within the chart border, then click the **Chart Type list arrow** on the Chart toolbar
    The chart type buttons appear, as shown in Figure 4-7.

4   Click the **2-D Pie Chart button** ⏣
    The column chart changes to a pie chart showing total sales by month (the *columns* in the selected range). See Figure 4-8. Evan looks at the pie chart and takes some notes, and then decides to convert it back to a column chart. He wants to see if the large increase in sales would be better presented with a three-dimensional column chart.

5   Click the Chart Type list arrow on the Chart toolbar, then click the **3-D Column Chart button** ⏣
    A three-dimensional column chart appears. The three-dimensional column format is too crowded, so Evan switches back to the two-dimensional format.

6   Click the Chart Type list arrow on the Chart toolbar, then click the **2-D Column Chart button** ⏣

TABLE 4-2: Chart type buttons

7   Click the **Save button** ⏣ on the Standard toolbar

BUTTON	DESCRIPTION	BUTTON	DESCRIPTION
⏣	Displays 2-D area chart	⏣	Displays 3-D area chart
⏣	Displays 2-D bar chart	⏣	Displays 3-D bar chart
⏣	Displays 2-D column chart	⏣	Displays 3-D column chart
⏣	Displays 2-D line chart	⏣	Displays 3-D line chart
⏣	Displays 2-D pie chart	⏣	Displays 3-D pie chart
⏣	Displays 2-D scatter chart	⏣	Displays 3-D surface chart
⏣	Displays 2-D doughnut chart	⏣	Displays radar chart

FIGURE 4-6: Worksheet with new data entered for the Northwest region

New data

Adjusted data points

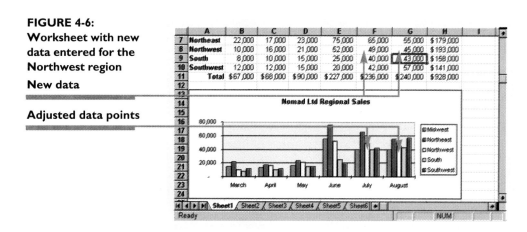

FIGURE 4-7: Chart Type list box

2-D Column Chart button

2-D Pie Chart button

3-D Column Chart button

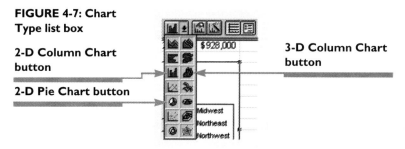

FIGURE 4-8: Pie chart

June sales pie slice

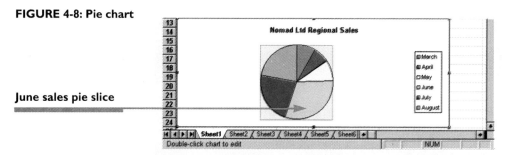

Rotating a chart

In a three-dimensional chart, columns or bars can sometimes be obscured by other data series within the same chart. You can rotate the chart until a better view is obtained. Double-click the chart, click the tip of one of its axes, then drag the handles until a more pleasing view of the data series appears. See Figure 4-9.

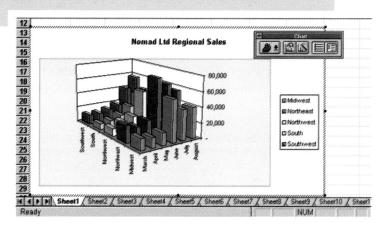

FIGURE 4-9: 3-D chart rotated with improved view of data series

Moving and resizing a chart and its objects

Charts are graphics, or drawn **objects**, and have no specific cell or range address. You can move charts anywhere on a worksheet without affecting formulas or data in the worksheet. You can even put them on another sheet. See the related topic "Viewing multiple worksheets" for more information. You can also easily resize a chart to improve its appearance by dragging the selection handles. Charts contain many elements—each is a separate object that you can move and resize. To move an object, select it then drag it or cut and copy it to a new location. To resize an object, use the selection handles. ▶ Evan wants to increase the size of the chart and center it on the worksheet. He also wants to move the legend up so that it is level with the title.

1 Select the **chart**, scroll the worksheet until row 31 is visible, then position the pointer over the bottom center selection handle until the pointer changes to ↕
   The pointer shape ↕ indicates that you can use a selection handle to resize the chart.

2 Press and hold the mouse button, drag the lower edge of the chart to row 31, then release the mouse button
   A dotted outline of the chart perimeter appears as the chart is being moved, and the pointer changes to ✛. The chart length is increased.

3 Position the pointer over one of the selection handles on the right, then drag the chart about 1/2" to the right to the middle of column I
   See Figure 4-10. Now, Evan moves the legend up so that it is level with the chart title.

4 Double-click the **chart**
   The chart is now in Edit mode. When the chart is in **Edit mode**, you can change elements within the chart border. When the chart is selected but not in Edit mode, you can move and resize the entire chart. In Edit mode, the border changes to a blue outline (shown in Figure 4-9) or the chart appears in its own window, and the menu bar changes to the Chart menu bar.

5 Click the **legend** to select it, then drag it to the upper-right corner of the chart until it is aligned with the chart title
   If the Chart toolbar is in the way of the legend, move it out of your way first. Selection handles appear around the legend when you click it, and a dotted outline of the legend perimeter appears as you drag. See Figure 4-11. Note that the floating Chart toolbar was moved to the other side of the window to move it out of the way of the repositioned legend.

6 Press **[Esc]** to deselect the legend

7 Click the **Save button** 🖫 on the Standard toolbar

FIGURE 4-10:
Worksheet with
resized and centered
chart

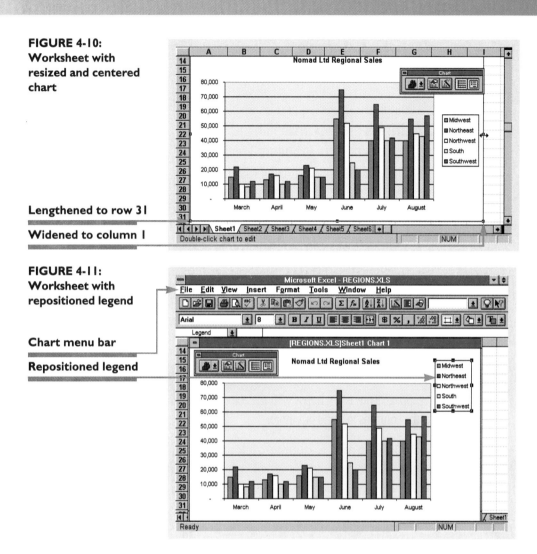

Lengthened to row 31

Widened to column I

FIGURE 4-11:
Worksheet with
repositioned legend

Chart menu bar

Repositioned legend

Viewing multiple worksheets

A workbook can be organized with a chart on one sheet and the data on another sheet. With this organization, you can still see the data next to the chart by opening multiple windows of the same workbook. This allows you to see portions of multiple sheets at the same time. Click Window on the menu bar, then click New Window. A new window containing the current workbook opens. To see the windows next to each other, click Window on the menu bar, click Arrange, then choose one of the options in the Arrange Windows dialog box. You can open one worksheet in one window and a different worksheet in the second window. See Figure 4-12. To close one window without closing the worksheet, double-click the control menu box on the window you want to close.

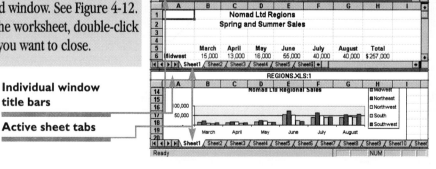

Individual window
title bars

Active sheet tabs

FIGURE 4-12: Workbook with two windows open

Changing the appearance of a chart

After you've created a chart using the ChartWizard, you can use the Chart toolbar to change the colors of data series, add or eliminate a legend, and add or delete gridlines. **Gridlines** are the horizontal lines in the chart that enable the eye to follow the value on an axis. These buttons are listed in Table 4-3. ▶ Evan wants to make some changes in the appearance of his chart. He wants to see if the chart looks better without gridlines, and he wants to change the color of a data series.

1. **Make sure the chart is still in Edit mode—that it has a blue border around it or is in its own window**
   Evan wants to see how the chart looks without gridlines. Currently gridlines appear and the Gridlines button 🗄 on the Chart toolbar is depressed.

2. **Click the Gridlines button 🗄 on the Chart toolbar**
   The gridlines disappear from the chart, and the button is deselected. Evan decides that the gridlines are necessary to the chart's readability.

3. **Click 🗄 again**
   The gridlines reappear. Evan is not happy with the color of the columns for the South data series and would like the columns to stand out more.

4. **With the chart in Edit mode, double-click any column in the South data series**
   Handles appear on all the columns in the series, and the Format Data Series dialog box opens, as shown in Figure 4-13. Make sure the Patterns tab is the front-most tab.

5. **Click the yellow box (in the first row, third from the right), then click OK**
   All the columns in the series are yellow. Compare your finished chart to Figure 4-14. Evan is pleased with the change.

6. **Click the Save button 🖫 on the Standard toolbar**

TABLE 4-3: Chart enhancement buttons

BUTTON	USE
🗄	Adds or deletes gridlines
🗄	Adds or deletes legend
🖎	Returns you to the ChartWizard

FIGURE 4-13: Format Data Series dialog box

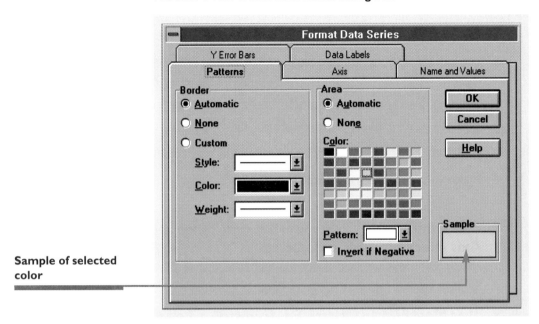

Sample of selected color

FIGURE 4-14: Chart with formatted data series

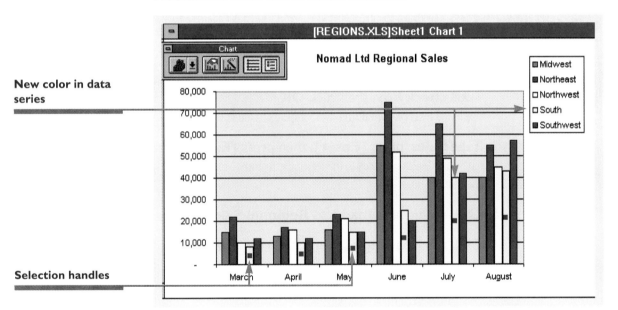

New color in data series

Selection handles

QUICK **TIP**

Experiment with different formats for your charts until you get just the right look.■

Enhancing a chart

There are many ways to enhance a chart to make it easier to read and understand. You can create titles for the x-axis and y-axis, add graphics, or add background color. You can even format the text you use in a chart. See the related topic "Changing text font and alignment in charts" for more information. ▶ Evan wants to improve the appearance of his chart by creating titles for the x-axis and y-axis. He also decides to add a drop shadow to the title.

1   **Make sure the chart is in Edit mode**
Evan wants to add descriptive text to the x-axis.

2   Click **Insert** on the Chart menu bar, click **Titles**, click the **Category (X) Axis check box**, then click **OK**
A text box with selection handles around it and containing an "X" appears below the x-axis, as shown in Figure 4-15.

3   Type **Months** then click the **Enter button** ⬜ on the formula bar
The word "Months" appears below the month labels. If you wanted to move the axis title to a new position, you could click on an edge of the selection and drag it. If you wanted to edit the axis title, position the pointer over the selected text box until it becomes I and click, then edit the text. Evan now adds text to the y-axis.

4   Click **Insert** on the Chart menu bar, click **Titles**, click the **Value (Y) Axis check box**, then click **OK**
A selected text box containing a "Y" appears to the left of the y-axis.

5   Type **Sales**, press **[Enter]**, then press **[Esc]** to deselect it
The word "Sales" appears to the left of the regions. Next Evan decides to add a drop shadow to the title.

6   Click the title **Nomad Ltd Regional Sales** to select it

7   Click the **Drawing button** ⬜ on the Standard toolbar
The Drawing toolbar appears.

8   Click the **Drop Shadow button** ⬜ on the Drawing toolbar, then press **[Esc]** to deselect the title
A drop shadow appears around the title. See Figure 4-16.

9   Click ⬜ then click the **Save button** ⬜ on the Standard toolbar
The Drawing toolbar no longer appears, and the chart is saved.

FIGURE 4-15: Chart with selected text box

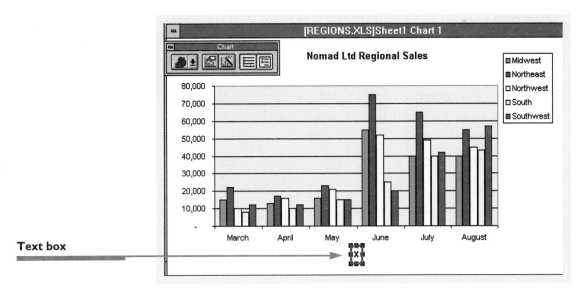

Text box

FIGURE 4-16: Enhanced chart

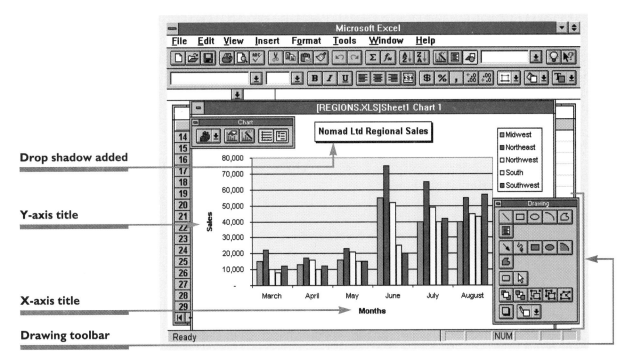

Drop shadow added

Y-axis title

X-axis title

Drawing toolbar

Changing text font and alignment in charts

The font and the alignment of axis text can be modified to make it more readable or to better fit within the plot area. With a chart in Edit mode, double-click the text to be modified. The Format Axis dialog box appears. Click the Font or the Alignment tab, make the desired changes, then click OK.

Adding text annotations and arrows to a chart

You can add arrows and text annotations to highlight information in your charts. **Text annotations** are labels that you add to a chart to draw attention to a certain part of it. See the related topic "Pulling out a pie slice" for another way to draw attention to a certain part of a chart. ▶ Evan wants to add a text annotation and an arrow to highlight the June sales increase.

1 **Make sure the chart is in Edit mode**
Evan wants to call attention to the June sales increase by drawing an arrow that points to the top of the June data series with the annotation, "After advertising campaign." To enter the text for an annotation, you simply start typing.

2 Type **After advertising campaign**, then click the **Enter button** ▢ on the formula bar
As you type, the text appears in the formula bar. After you confirm the entry, the text appears in a selected text box within the chart window. See Figure 4-17. Your text box might be in a different location on your screen.

3 **Point to an edge of the text box, then press and hold the left mouse button**
The pointer should be �!�, and the message in the status bar should say "Move selected objects." If the pointer changes to I or ↔, release the mouse button, click outside the text box area to deselect it, then select the text box and repeat Step 3.

4 **Drag the text box above the chart, as shown in Figure 4-18, then release the mouse button**
Evan is ready to add an arrow.

5 Click the **Drawing button** ▨ on the Standard toolbar
The Drawing toolbar appears.

6 Click the **Arrow button** ◲ on the Drawing toolbar
The pointer changes to +.

7 Position + under the word **campaign** in the text box, click the **left mouse button**, drag the line to the June sales, then release the mouse button
An arrowhead appears pointing to the June sales. Compare your finished chart to Figure 4-18.

8 Close the Drawing toolbar then click the **Save button** ▤ on the Standard toolbar

FIGURE 4-17: Chart with new text box

Drawing button

Move text box here

Selected floating text box

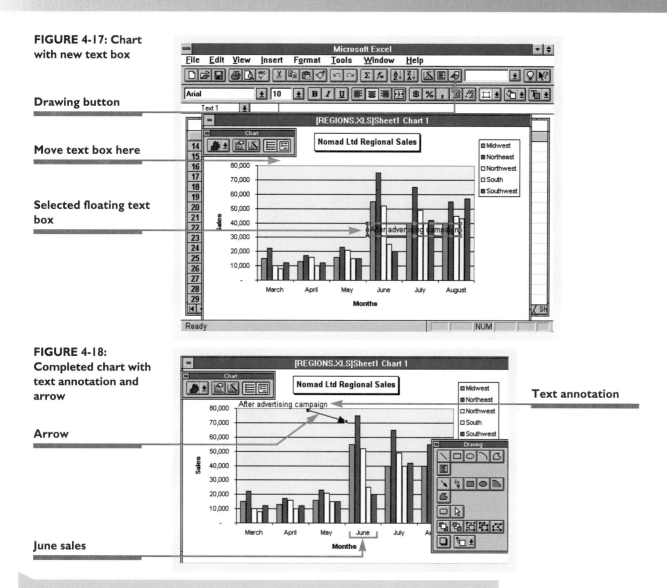

FIGURE 4-18: Completed chart with text annotation and arrow

Arrow

June sales

Text annotation

Pulling out a pie slice

Just as an arrow can call attention to a data series, you can emphasize a pie slice by **exploding** it, or pulling it away, from the pie chart. Once the chart is in Edit mode, click the pie to select it, click the desired slice to select only the slice, then drag the slice away from the pie, as shown in Figure 4-19.

FIGURE 4-19: Exploded pie slice

Slice pulled from pie

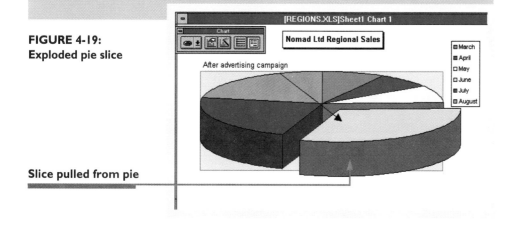

QUICK **TIP**

You can insert text and an arrow in the data section of a worksheet by clicking the Text Box button ▦ on the Standard toolbar, drawing a text box, then typing the text and then adding the arrow.◼

Previewing and printing a chart

After you complete a chart to your satisfaction, you will need to print it. You can print a chart by itself, or as part of the worksheet. ▶ Evan is satisfied with the chart and wants to print it for the Annual Meeting. He will print the worksheet and the chart together, so that the shareholders can see the actual sales numbers for each tour type.

1   Click in any cell outside the chart to turn off Edit mode, then click outside the chart to deselect it
    If you wanted to print only the chart without the data, you would leave the chart in Edit mode.

2   Click the **Print Preview button** 🔍 on the Standard toolbar
    The Print Preview window opens. Evan decides that the chart and data would look better if they were printed in **landscape** orientation—that is, with the page turned sideways. To change the orientation of the page, you must alter the page setup.

3   Click **Setup** to display the Page Setup dialog box, then click the **Page tab**

4   Click the **Landscape radio button** in the Orientation section
    See Figure 4-20. Evan would also like to eliminate the gridlines that appear in the data.

5   Click the **Sheet tab** then click the **Gridlines check box** to deselect it
    The chart and data will print too far over to the left of the page. Evan changes this using the Margins tab.

6   Click the **Margins tab**, double-click the **Left text box**, type **2.25**, then click **OK**
    The print preview of the worksheet appears again. The data and chart are centered on the page that is turned sideways, and no gridlines appear. See Figure 4-21. Evan is satisfied with the way it looks and prints it.

7   Click **Print** to display the Print dialog box, then click **OK**
    Your printed report should look like the image displayed in the Print Preview window.

8   Click the **Save button** 💾 on the Standard toolbar, click **File** on the menu bar, then click **Close**
    Your workbook and chart close.

9   Click **File** on the menu bar, then click **Exit** to exit Excel and return to the Program Manager

FIGURE 4-20: Page tab of the Page Setup dialog box

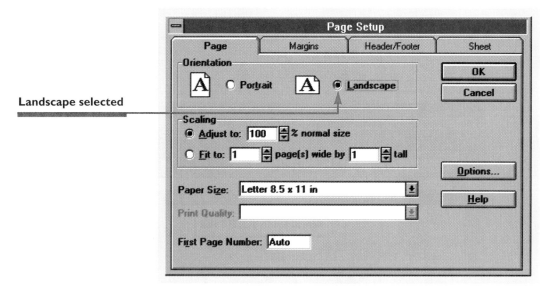

Landscape selected

FIGURE 4-21: Chart and data ready to print

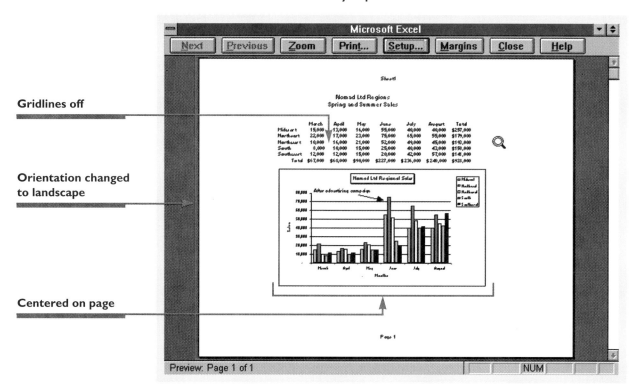

Gridlines off

Orientation changed
to landscape

Centered on page

QUICK **TIP**

You can print charts
and worksheets on
transparencies for use
on an overhead
projector.■

CONCEPTSREVIEW

Label each of the elements of the Excel chart shown in Figure 4-22.

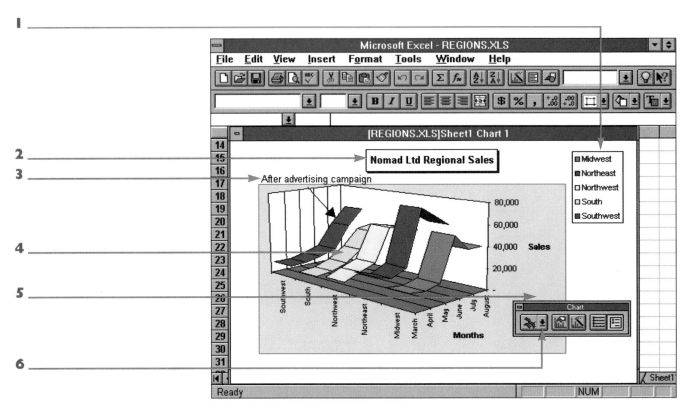

FIGURE 4-22

Match each of the statements with its chart type.

7 Shows how volume changes over time

8 Compares data as parts of a whole

9 Displays a column and line chart using different scales of measurement

10 Compares trends over even time intervals

11 Compares data over time— the Excel default

a. Column

b. Area

c. Pie

d. Combination

e. Line

Select the best answer from the list of choices.

12 The box that identifies patterns used for each data series is a

a. Data point

b. Plot

c. Legend

d. Range

13 What is the term for a row or column on a chart?

a. Range address

b. Axis titles

c. Chart orientation

d. Data series

14 The first step when creating a chart is to

a. Click Chart on the Insert menu

b. Select a cell

c. Select a range

d. Click the ChartWizard button on the Standard toolbar

15 The button used to add a drop shadow is

a. ▤

b. ▣

c. ▣

d. ◥

APPLICATIONSREVIEW

1 Create a distribution report worksheet, then create a column chart.

a. Start Excel, open a new workbook, then save it as SOFTWARE.XLS to the MY_FILES directory on your Student Disk.

b. Enter the information from Table 4-4 in your worksheet in range A1..F6. Resize columns and rows as necessary.

TABLE 4-4

	Excel	Word	WordPerfect	PageMaker
Accounting	10	1	9	0
Marketing	2	9	0	6
Engineering	12	5	7	1
Personnel	2	2	2	1
Production	6	3	4	0

c. Save your work.

d. Select all the entered information, then click the ChartWizard button.

e. Select the range in the worksheet where you want to insert the chart.

f. Complete the ChartWizard dialog boxes and build a two-dimensional column chart with a different color bar for each department and with the title "Software Distribution by Department."

g. Drag the selection handles of the chart so it fills your screen.

h. Save your work.

2 Edit a chart and change the chart type.

a. Change the value in cell B3 to 6 .

b. Select the chart by clicking on it.

c. Click the Chart Type list arrow on the Chart toolbar.

d. Click the 3-D Column Chart button in the list.

e. Save your work.

3 Add a text annotation and an arrow to the current chart.

a. Double-click the chart to put it in Edit mode.

b. Create the text annotation "Need More Computers."

c. Drag the text annotation about 1" above any of the Personnel bars.

d. Click the Arrow button on the Draw toolbar.

e. Click below the text annotation, drag down to the top of any one of the Personnel bars, then release the mouse button.

f. Add arrows from the text annotation to each of the remaining Personnel bars.

g. Save your work.

4 Enhance a chart.

a. Make sure the chart is still in Edit mode, then click Insert on the menu bar, click Titles, click the Category (X) Axis check box, then click OK.

b. Type "Department" in the selected text box below the x-axis, then click the Enter button on the formula bar.

c. Click Insert on the menu bar, click Titles, select Value (Y) Series check box, then click OK.

d. Type "Types of Software" in the selected text box to the left of the y-axis, then click the Enter button on the formula bar.

e. Save your work.

5 Change the appearance of a chart.

a. Make sure the chart is still in Edit mode.

b. Click the Gridlines button on the Chart toolbar.

c. Save your work.

6 Move and resize a chart object.

a. Make sure the chart is still in Edit mode.

b. Click the legend to select it.

c. Drag the selection handles to make the legend larger and wider by about 1/2".

d. Move the legend below the charted data.

e. Save your work.

7 Preview and print a chart.

a. Make sure the chart is still in Edit mode, then click the Print Preview button on the Standard toolbar.

b. Center the chart on the page and change the paper orientation to landscape.

c. Click Print in the Print Preview window.

d. Save your work, close the workbook, then exit Excel.

INDEPENDENT
CHALLENGE 1

You are the operations manager for the Springfield Municipal Recycling Center. The Marketing Department wants you to create charts for a brochure that will advertise a new curbside recycling program. The data provided contains percentages of all collected recycled goods. Using this data, you need to create charts that show:

- How much of each type of recycled material Springfield collected in 1994 and what percentage of the whole each type represents. The center collects all types of paper, plastics, and glass from both business and residential customers.

- The yearly increases in the total amounts of recycled materials the center has collected since its inception three years ago. Springfield has experienced a 30% annual increase in collections.

To complete this independent challenge:

1 Prepare a worksheet plan that states your goal and identifies the formulas for any calculations.

2 Sketch a sample worksheet on a piece of paper describing how you will create the charts. Which type of chart is best suited for the information you need to display? What kind of chart enhancements will be necessary? Will a 3-D effect make your chart easier to understand?

3 Open the workbook UNIT_4-2.XLS on your Student Disk, then save it as RECYCLE.XLS to the MY_FILES directory.

4 Add a column that calculates the 30% increase in annual collections.

5 Create at least six different charts that show the distribution of recycled goods, as well as the distribution by customer type. Use the ChartWizard to switch the way data is plotted (columns vs. rows and vice versa) to come up with additional charts. Make sure your charts show the information requested above.

6 After creating the charts, make the appropriate enhancements. Include chart titles, legends, and axis titles.

7 Before printing, preview the file so you know what the charts will look like. Adjust any items as needed.

8 Print the charts without printing the data. Then print a copy of the entire worksheet. Save your work before closing the file.

9 Submit your worksheet plan, preliminary sketches, and the final worksheet printouts.

INDEPENDENT
CHALLENGE 2

As an administrator with the US Census Bureau, you are concerned with the distribution of the population by age and gender. Using the statistical data provided below, you need to create charts that show:

- How the population is distributed, by age and gender
- How the population is distributed, by gender

AGE	MALE	FEMALE
65+	5%	7.5%
55-64	4%	4.5%
45-54	4.9%	5.2%
35-44	7.4%	7.6%
25-34	8.7%	8.7%
15-24	7.6%	7.3%
5-14	7.2%	6.9%
<5	3.9%	3.7%

To complete this independent challenge:

1 Prepare a worksheet plan that states your goal and identifies the formulas for any calculations.

2 Sketch a sample worksheet on a piece of paper describing how you will create the charts. Which type of charts are best suited for the information you need to display? What kind of chart enhancements will be necessary? Will a 3-D effect make your chart easier to understand?

3 Open a new workbook using the data above, and save it as CENSUS.XLS to the MY_FILES directory on your Student Disk.

4 Create at least six different charts that show the population in its entirety, by gender, by age, and by both gender and age. Use the ChartWizard to switch the way data is plotted (columns vs. rows and vice versa) to come up with additional charts. Make sure your charts show the information requested above.

5 Add annotated text and arrows highlighting any data you feel is particularly important. Change colors to emphasize significant data.

6 Before printing, preview the file so you know what the charts will look like. Adjust any items as needed.

7 Print the charts with the data. Save your work before closing the file.

8 Submit your worksheet plan, preliminary sketches, and the final worksheet printouts.

Glossary

Absolute reference   A cell reference that contains a dollar sign before the column letter and/or row number to indicate the absolute, or fixed, contents of specific cells. For example, the formula $A$1+$B$1 calculates only the sum of these specific cells.

Active cell   The cell in which you are working, indicated by the current location of the cell pointer.

Address   The location of a specific cell or range expressed by the coordinates of column and row; for example, A1.

Alignment   The horizontal placement of cell contents; for example, left, center, or right.

Anchors   Cells listed in a range address. For example, in the formula =SUM(A1:A15), A1 and A15 are anchors.

Area chart   A line chart in which each area is given a solid color or pattern to emphasize the relationships between the pieces of charted information.

Argument   A value, range of cells, or text used in a macro or function. An argument is enclosed in parentheses; for example, =SUM(A1..B1).

Arithmetic operator   A symbol used in formulas, such as + or –, to perform calculations.

Attributes   The styling features such as bold, italics, and underlining that can be applied to cell contents.

AutoFormat   A feature that provides preset schemes that can be applied to instantly format a range. Excel comes with sixteen AutoFormats, which include colors, fonts, and numeric formatting.

Bar chart   The bar chart displays information as a series of (horizontal) bars.

Button   A picture on a toolbar that represents a shortcut for performing a commonly used Excel command. For example, you can click the Save button to save a file.

Cancel button   The button pictured with an "X" on it located on the formula bar. The Cancel button removes the changes made to the contents of the active cell and restores the previous cell contents.

Cell   The intersection of a column and a row.

Cell address   Unique location identified by intersecting column and row coordinates.

Cell pointer   A highlighted rectangle around a cell that indicates the active cell.

Cell reference   The address or name of a specific cell; cell references can be used in formulas and are relative or absolute.

Chart   A graphic representation of selected worksheet information. Types include 2-D and 3-D column, bar, pie, area, and line charts.

Chart title   The name assigned to a chart.

ChartWizard   A feature that provides a series of dialog boxes that help create or modify a chart.

Check box   A square box in a dialog box that you click to turn an option on or off.

Clear   A command used to erase a cell's contents, formatting, or both.

Clipboard   A temporary storage area for cut or copied data and graphics. You can paste the contents of the Clipboard into any Excel worksheet or open Excel workbook. The Clipboard holds the information until you cut or copy another piece of data or graphic.

Close   A command that puts a file away but keeps Excel open so that you can continue to work on other workbooks.

Column chart   The default chart type in Excel. The column chart displays information as a series of (vertical) columns.

Column selector button   The gray box containing the column letter above the column.

Copy   A command that copies the selected information and places it on the Clipboard.

Cut   A command that removes the contents from a selected area of a worksheet and places them on the Clipboard, so you can paste the selected text in another worksheet or open workbook.

Data marker   Visible representation of a data point, such as a column or pie slice.

Data point   Individual piece of data plotted in a chart.

Data series   The selected range in a worksheet that Excel converts into a graphic and displays as a chart.

Delete   A command that removes cell contents from a worksheet.

Dialog box   A window that displays when you choose a command whose name is followed by an ellipsis (...). A dialog box allows you to make selections that determine how the command affects the selected area.

Drag-and-drop   A way of moving or copying cells, rows, and columns by dragging the data with the mouse to a new worksheet location.

Drive   A mechanism in a computer or an area of a network used for retrieving and storing files. Personal computers usually have one hard disk drive labeled C and two drives labeled A and B that read removable floppy disks.

Dummy column/row   Blank column or row included at the end of a range that enables a formula to adjust when columns or rows are added or deleted.

Edit   Add, delete, or change the contents of a cell or worksheet.

Electronic spreadsheet   A computer program that performs calculations on data and organizes information. A spreadsheet is divided into columns and rows that form individual cells.

Ellipsis   A series of dots (...) following a command, indicating that more choices are available through a dialog box.

Enter button   The button pictured with a checkmark on it located on the formula bar. The Enter button is used to confirm an entry to the active cell.

Exploding pie slice   A slice of a pie chart that has been pulled away from a pie to add emphasis.

Fill Down   A command that duplicates the contents of the selected cells in the range selected below the cell pointer.

Fill handle   Small square in the lower-right corner of the active cell used to copy cell contents.

Fill right   A command that duplicates the contents of the selected cells in the range selected to the right of the cell pointer.

Font   The name given to a collection of characters (letters, numerals, symbols, and punctuation marks) with a specific design. Arial and Times New Roman are examples of font names.

Format   The way text and numbers appear on a worksheet. *See also* Number format.

Formula   A set of instructions that you enter in a cell to perform numeric calculations (adding, multiplying, averaging, etc.); for example, +A1+B1.

Formula bar   The rectangular area, above the Excel worksheet window, that displays a cell's contents, including numbers, text, and formulas, when you click a cell. You can use the formula bar to enter and edit data in the active cell.

Function   A special predefined worksheet formula that provides a shortcut for commonly used calculations; for example, AVERAGE. A function always begins with the formula prefix = (the equal sign).

Function Wizard   A feature that provides a series of dialog boxes that list and describe all Excel functions and assists the user in function creation.

Gridlines   Horizontal lines within a chart that make the chart easier to read.

Input   Information that produces desired results in a worksheet.

Insertion point   Blinking vertical line that appears in the formula bar during entry and editing.

Label   Descriptive text or other information that identifies the rows and columns of a worksheet. Labels are not included in calculations.

Landscape   Term used to refer to printing across the wider dimension of a page, generally 11" horizontally by 8 ½" vertically.

Legend   A key explaining the information represented by colors or patterns in a chart.

Line chart   A graph of data that is mapped by a series of lines. Line charts show changes in data or categories of data over time and can be used to document trends.

Menu bar   The horizontal bar under the title bar on a window that lists the names of the menus that contain Excel commands. Click a menu name on the menu bar to display a list of commands.

Mode indicator   A box located on the far left of the status bar that informs you of the program's status. For example, when Excel is performing a task, the word "Wait" appears in the mode indicator.

Mouse pointer   An arrow that indicates the current location of the mouse on the desktop. The mouse pointer changes shapes at times depending on the application and task being executed or performed.

Name box   The leftmost area on the formula bar that shows the name or address of the area currently selected. For example, "A1" refers to cell A1 of the current worksheet.

Number format   A format applied to values to express numeric concepts, such as currency, date, and percent.

Object   A chart or graphic image that can be moved and resized and contains handles when selected.

Open   A command that retrieves a workbook from a disk and displays it on the screen.

Order of precedence   The order in which Excel calculates parts of a formula: (1) exponents, (2) multiplication and division, and (3) addition and subtraction.

Output   The end result of a worksheet.

Paste   A command that moves information on the Clipboard to a new location. Excel pastes the formulas rather than the result unless the Paste Special command is used.

Paste Special   A command that enables you to paste formulas as values, styles, or cell contents.

Pie chart   A circular chart that displays data as slices of a pie. A pie chart is useful for showing the relationship of parts to a whole; pie slices can be pulled away, or exploded, from the pie for emphasis.

Point size   Refers to the physical size of text, measured in points. One inch equals 72 points.

Print Preview   A window that displays a reduced view of area to be printed.

Radio button   Circle in a dialog box that allows you to choose one option from a list of options.

Range   A selected group of adjacent cells.

Range format   A format applied to a selected range in a worksheet.

Range name   A name applied to a selected range in a worksheet.

Relative cell reference   Used to indicate a relative position in the worksheet. This allows you to copy and move formulas from one area to another of the same dimensions. Excel automatically changes the column and row numbers to reflect the new position.

Row height   The vertical dimension of a cell.

Row selector button   Gray box containing the row number to the left of the row.

Save   A command used to save incremental changes to a workbook.

Save As   A command used to create a duplicate of the current workbook.

Scroll bars   Bars that appear on the right and bottom borders of the window that allow you to scroll the window vertically and horizontally to view information not currently visible in the current worksheet.

Search criteria   Text, values, or formulas you want to change using Find and Replace.

Selection handles   Small black boxes at the corners and sides of charts and graphic images, indicating a chart is selected and can be moved or resized using the handles.

Sheet tab   A description at the bottom of each worksheet that identifies the sheet in a workbook. In an open workbook, move to a worksheet by clicking its tab.

Sheet tab scrolling buttons   Enable you to move among sheets within a workbook.

Status bar   The horizontal bar at the bottom of the Excel window that provides information about the tasks Excel is performing or about current selections.

Text annotations   Labels added to a chart to draw attention to a particular area.

Title bar   The horizontal bar at the top of a window that displays the application name and workbook. Until you save the workbook and give it a name, the temporary name for the workbook is BOOK1.

Toggle button   A choice that, when clicked, turns an option on. Clicking it again turns the option off.

Toolbar   A horizontal bar within the Excel window that contains buttons for the most frequently used Excel commands. A toolbar can be positioned along the edge of the worksheet window or can float within its own window.

ToolTip   Name and description of a button on the toolbar that appears when the mouse pointer is positioned over the button. The name appears under the button and the description in the status bar.

Values   Numbers, formulas, or functions used in calculations.

"What-if" analysis   Decision-making feature in which data is changed and automatically recalculated.

Workbook   A collection of related worksheets contained within a single file.

Worksheet   An electronic spreadsheet containing 256 columns by 16,384 rows.

Worksheet window   A framed area of the Excel window containing a grid of columns and rows that is called a worksheet.

X-axis   The horizontal line in a chart.

X-axis label   A label describing the x-axis of a chart.

Y-axis   The vertical line in a chart.

Y-axis label   A label describing the y-axis of a chart.

Zoom   A feature that enables you to focus on a larger or smaller part of the worksheet in Print Preview.

Index